50
GREAT TREES
of the National Trust

50
GREAT TREES
of the National Trust

SIMON TOOMER

National Trust

Contents

Introduction

Within the gardens, parks and countryside properties owned and cared for by the National Trust grow some of the oldest, largest, rarest and sometimes most endangered trees in cultivation. They vary from mighty conifers to delicate ornamental broadleaves, reflecting the range of habitats, landscapes and climates in which they live. Many are representatives of our native flora, living reminders of Britain's wild woodland, traditional land-management practices or long-forgotten landscapes. Ancient veterans such as the Old Man of Calke and the pollarded hornbeams of Hatfield Forest have lived through many centuries of change and they have, literally, been shaped by their interaction with humans. Other trees have more exotic and recent origins and have been planted here for ornamental or productive purposes. Britain is poorly endowed with native trees in comparison to mainland Europe, and the contrast is even greater with botanical hotspots such as China, Japan and South America. Only around 30 tree species managed to recolonise our shores in the wake of the receding ice sheets after the last glacial period. Flooding of the English Channel around 10,000 years ago effectively slammed the door to slower or less hardy latecomers, and the list of true natives was fixed. Our rich tree heritage is therefore down to centuries of human collection, introduction and cultivation.

The Romans are thought to have been the first to introduce southern European trees such as walnut and sweet chestnut for their nutritious nuts, but it was the needs and acquisitive instincts of later generations of foresters, gardeners and plantspeople that so enriched our countryside and garden treescapes with thousands more species. Fast-growing conifers and versatile broadleaves have complemented native species such as oak, elm and Scots pine for constructing buildings and ships and fuelling homes and factories.

Trees in the landscape

Over time, trees increasingly came to be valued for their aesthetic qualities and their unique

Opposite · An autumnal view of Newton House and the 18th-century landscape park at Dinefwr, Carmarthenshire.

Frontispiece · Sycamore Gap, Hadrian's Wall, Northumberland: this strikingly sited tree is one of the Trust's most photographed.

Pages 4–5 · The imposing cork oak, a county champion, at Osterley Park, Middlesex.

ability to help shape garden and parkland landscapes, providing both continuity and seasonal variety. Many gardens of medieval origin had to make do with a restricted palette of primarily native trees. Yew, box, holly and other evergreens were used to define and subdivide gardens and to provide formal or geometrical structure. The garden at Montacute House (left), for example, still betrays its Jacobean origins through the framework of yews and other native evergreens. Formality and rigid structure continued to be the order of the day in French Renaissance gardens of the 17th century, with trees used as the servants of design rather than as living things to be admired in their own right. The Glorious Revolution of 1688 loosened the links with France and helped release gardens and their trees from the rigid constraints of straight lines and pruned discipline. Dutch influences brought a more relaxed approach, although gardens of this period such as Erddig and Westbury Court retain formal elements, with trees serving both structural and naturalistic purposes.

The late 18th century saw the rise of the English Landscape Garden style and the ambition to garden on a massive scale.

Left · View along the west drive of the 16th-century house and formal gardens at Montacute, Somerset.

emphasise and complement architectural and other designed features, so species choice was essential. At Ickworth, Mediterranean pines and cypresses enhance the Italianate Garden's classical 'vibe' and set the scene for the famous Rotunda. Holm oak was also a popular tree to frame and soften the outlines of temples and grottoes like those at Stourhead.

Trees, either individually or in clumps or avenues, were an essential component in these landscapes and the growing palette of readily available trees conveniently coincided with this monumental change in garden fashion. Species such as cedar of Lebanon and Oriental plane, quite unlike any of our native species, would have caused quite a frisson of excitement and helped contemporary designers such as Lancelot 'Capability' Brown (1716–83) and Humphry Repton (1752–1818) (above) to realise fantastic landscapes inspired by classical visions of perfection. As well as being landscape features in their own right, trees could

As with all fashions, the English Landscape Gardens of Brown, Repton and others came, in time, to be regarded as old hat. The perfect curves and tended lawns were criticised for being overly formal and contrived. An alternative, more naturalistic style gained favour, promoted by William Gilpin (1724–1804), Uvedale Price (1747–1829) and other influential artists and writers of the day. The new Picturesque style also emphasised the value of the trees themselves rather than their supporting role. Price favoured the wild and unkempt aspects of landscape and what he described as the 'accidents of nature'. Trees, including fallen or withered ones, were seen as valuable contributors to the overall Picturesque

effect, essential for the 'infinite variety in their forms, tints ... light and shade'.

Estate owners, convinced of the merits of the new Picturesque style, could call on the services of landscape 'improvers' to help bring their gardens and parks up to date. William Sawrey Gilpin (1762–1843), nephew of William Gilpin, was one such adviser, whose work can be admired at a number of National Trust gardens and parks, including Scotney Castle, Clumber Park (overleaf) and Beningbrough Hall. W.S. Gilpin was primarily a landscape artist with little knowledge of trees but he

had an acute sense of how different shapes, habit and texture could contribute to achieving the desired qualities of intricacy, variety and connection. Recognising that the writing was on the wall for the earlier Brownian style, Humphry Repton quickly embraced the new fashion and adopted Picturesque principles in the use of trees in his later plans for gardens such as Sheringham Park (above and pages 216–7).

For the owners of some properties, trees assumed a symbolic role with religious or political meanings. At Tyntesfield, the Gibbs family expressed their Anglo-Catholicism

through architecture and commissioned works of art (overleaf). Clues to their religious affiliation were often included in these artefacts in the form of stylised plant symbols with Christian significance. They also planted trees with links to the holy lands, including a cedar collected during a visit to Lebanon. The tree can still be seen growing in the Paradise arboretum at Tyntesfield.

For many of the creators and owners of the great houses and gardens of the 18th and 19th centuries, plants, and trees in particular, were desirable acquisitions and collectables in their own right. The arboretum became a popular contemporary feature of large estates, often distinct from other landscape components such as the pleasure grounds and park. They were places to display one's most impressive tree acquisitions, especially conifers, and the term pinetum was often used to describe them. Humphry Repton included an arboretum in his 1815 plan for Ashridge Park alongside other features, including a pomarium and a rosarium. In the 19th century, arboretums readily lent themselves to the Victorian fashion for ordering and displaying nature in a systematic and rational scientific way. They represented a

Left • View of the lake, Chapel and treescape at Clumber Park, Nottinghamshire.

global excursion through a selection of trees to be found across the expanding British Empire, and Benjamin Disraeli was clearly inspired by this mood when planting the tree collection around the house and in the pleasure grounds at Hughenden.

In 20th-century gardens, tree choice often became more restrained. Arts and Crafts gardens such as Sissinghurst and Hidcote tended to favour small flowering and domesticated trees such as cherries and apples to create an atmosphere of intimate 'homely' familiarity rather than grandeur and ambition. However, smaller scale does not equate to less diversity and the 20th century saw continuing growth in the appetite of gardeners for choice and variety. In particular, plant breeders responded to the demand for small trees for modest spaces with a wealth of new and attractive varieties. Trees such as Japanese maples, cherries and dwarf conifers have become popular for their adaptability to small urban spaces and their availability in a variety of colours and shapes. These qualities are utilised in the more intimate National Trust gardens, where beauty can be appreciated up close.

Right • Detail of a mosaic panel (*c*.1875), one of a series of triptychs made by Salviati & Co. and designed by H.E. Wooldridge, in the Chapel at Tyntesfield, North Somerset.

Tree treasures

For passionate plant collectors such as Reginald Cory (1871–1934) of Dyffryn House (overleaf), trees were the living equivalents of the property's indoor artefacts – chinoiserie with leaves. The arboretum at Dyffryn is like an outdoor gallery of his tree acquisitions, many of which were among the first of their kind to be grown in Britain. Dyffryn's surviving mature specimens provide a direct link with the manic period of Victorian and Edwardian plant collecting, when the foremost nurseries of the day competed with one another to satisfy their wealthy clientele's demand for novel plants. Hired botanists and 'plant hunters' were dispatched on perilous missions with instructions not to return empty-handed. Collectors such as William Lobb (1809–64) and Robert Fortune (1812–80) became revered figures in the world of plant collecting, and some of their original trees can still be seen growing in National Trust gardens, including Killerton and Biddulph Grange. The expansion of plant availability did not occur in isolation but went hand-in-hand with exploration, discovery and European colonisation of an increasing area of the globe. The discovery of each new continent or region brought with it new and exciting botanical booty. Political manipulation also played its part in making plants available, just as it did with other resources. Much of Japan's great plant diversity, for example, only became available to European growers once a more Western-friendly regime was established late in the 19th century.

Unnatural selection

The quest for new plants didn't stop with the acquisition of wild species. From this botanical 'raw material', plant breeders have created a rich heritage of cultivated varieties to meet every taste and garden application. Sometimes these desirable forms come about through serendipitous hybridisation when previously geographically separate but closely related plants are brought together in cultivation. More often they arise from careful selection and breeding by enthusiasts with an obsessive eye for detail. Subtle natural differences in colour, shape, pattern or size provide the grist for this artificial evolutionary mill and open up the possibility of propagating cloned offspring that emphasise the most desirable characteristics. Thus cultivated plants such as copper beech and weeping ash end up looking very different from their wild counterparts, just as a lapdog bears little resemblance to a wolf. Some garden owners became besotted with a particular group of trees and their gardens became 'showrooms' of their adoration: the rhododendrons of Cragside and the magnolias of Lanhydrock are examples.

Spanning centuries of landscape and horticultural heritage, National Trust gardens and parks together represent a unique timeline of tree introduction and cultivation. And as well as hosting plants originating elsewhere, Trust gardens themselves have been fertile horticultural melting pots from which new varieties of trees have arisen through hybridisation or selection. Many garden creators and owners were among the horticultural 'movers and shakers' of their day and they employed the best gardeners and plantspeople to help realise their ambitions. Many of the distinctive plant varieties they selected are now named and forever associated with the property or its owner. The Messel family of Nymans were avid gardeners, plant collectors and breeders, and a number of varieties of magnolia and other trees and shrubs are named after the garden or acknowledge members of the family. The stunningly beautiful small tree *Eucryphia x nymansensis* 'Nymansay' (overleaf) can be seen in many gardens but is best appreciated in the walled garden at Nymans where it originated.

Right · The Paved Court in August at Dyffryn House and Gardens, Vale of Glamorgan. The rich and diverse range of plants and trees here and elsewhere at Dyffryn reflects a period of avid plant collecting by former owner Reginald Cory.

The 50 trees featured in this book

Selecting just 50 great trees was both an interesting and a daunting task. It would be easy to fill a book like this many times over with just the largest, the oldest or the rarest trees growing at National Trust places. Instead, the intention has been to select representatives of this vast and diverse tree heritage and, in particular, those with the best stories to tell. As well as being fascinating living organisms in their own right, trees often provide an entry point from which to understand the history and culture of a particular time and place. The planting and tending of trees is intimately woven into the material, cultural and aesthetic fabric of places and the people who have inhabited them. It is no wonder then that trees are a reflection of these inhabitants' needs, passions, fashions and interests.

Trees such as Newton's Apple Tree at Woolsthorpe Manor and the Martyrs' Sycamore at Tolpuddle have acquired great individual significance and provide a tangible link with monumental moments in science and social history. Others represent more general but no less significant change or events. Sitka spruce, grown as an ornamental tree in Victorian forest gardens such as Aira Force, was later planted by the million in the uplands of Britain to provide a strategic reserve of timber following the ravaging of woodlands for pit props, temporary buildings and other essential uses during the two world wars. Some trees were selected for the link they provide between trees and the products of their wood. House collections often include exquisite pieces of furniture or fittings made from beautifully grained timbers. Walnut and lime were especially valued by cabinet-makers and carvers respectively, and at Antony House in Cornwall a wonderful black walnut tree in the garden provides a link with pieces of 18th-century walnut furniture within the house.

Trees were also chosen to provide geographical spread so that visitors to National Trust places in all regions can look out for them. The gazetteer section at the end of this book provides a brief location description to help contextualise each selected tree. It also includes other gardens and parks where great trees can be seen. A few of the selections are not individuals but trees in avenues or groups, where their landscape significance and story is a collective one.

All the trees, which are presented here in no particular order, can be appreciated and enjoyed at any time of year. Some of them, however, such as the handkerchief tree or magnolias, are known for seasonal highlights of flowers, fruit or foliage colour. Guidance on when best to see such trees is included in the summary information that follows each tree entry, alongside the tree's botanical name,

plant family, habit and, for non-native species, its area of origin. Inevitably, the extent of this information varies considerably from one entry to another since it isn't always known or available. Inevitably, too, the selection of 50 trees that follows, passes over some highly significant examples that are no less important for their omission. These include the 2,500-year-old Ankerwycke Yew, the oldest tree cared for by the National Trust, which is vulnerable to damage from increased visitor numbers so has been left out of the spotlight here.

The story continues

National Trust gardens represent well over 400 years of horticultural and garden history and tradition. However, they are not static creations and they have changed over time in response to shifting economics, fashions and the fortunes of their owners. This is equally true of the trees that grow within them and indeed the one certain thing about all trees is that they will one day die. Conservation, therefore, means not just caring for today's trees but timely planting of their eventual replacements. A tree takes a long time to mature and play its part in the garden landscape, so gardeners and foresters need to think at least

50 years ahead. As well as the attrition of time, storms and other perturbations of weather, and increasing threats from a changing climate and tree diseases mean that tree collections need to adapt to survive. Balancing the need to maintain the historical spirit of place created by the established palette of trees alongside the need for greater climate and disease resilience requires careful species selection.

Like their predecessors, trees planted today will continue to illustrate and reflect the world around them and commemorate contemporary events of local, national and international significance. In May 2021 the National Trust contributed to the planting of 33 blossom trees arranged in three circles at London's Olympic Park to commemorate the lives lost during the Covid-19 pandemic, and to pay tribute to the key workers involved in health and other essential services.

A bigger picture

As well as incorporating new species and cultivars into traditional garden landscapes to ensure their health and resilience, the Trust contributes to wider national and international initiatives for the conservation of wild and cultivated trees. Tree collections and arboretums originally planted for ornament or ostentatious display have taken on a

Opposite (left) · The Plant Conservation Centre, Devon, which was set up to help conserve the rich diversity of plants at National Trust places.

Opposite (right) · Grafted apple trees grown to conserve traditional garden varieties.

Overleaf · Aerial view of woodland at Ringwood Toll, Sheffield Park, East Sussex.

contemporary conservation purpose. At High Close Arboretum in Cumbria endangered conifers have been planted as part of the International Conifer Conservation Programme. These tree equivalents of the giant panda can be seen growing among more familiar Lakeland trees such as coast and giant redwoods, planted in the 19th century when they were, themselves, the latest tree novelties. Some new tree species have even been discovered since our gardens were first planted, and by growing them alongside trees first planted in the 18th or 19th centuries we continue a tradition begun by the enthusiastic plantspeople of that era. Wollemi pine, for example, discovered growing in a remote gorge in New South Wales in 1994, can now be seen in a number of National Trust gardens, including Winkworth Arboretum in Surrey.

Our gardens also play an important role in conserving old varieties of trees, such as apples and pears that have fallen out of favour. In 2016, the Trust stepped in to help conserve over 300 traditional West Country cider apple varieties through propagation and cultivation in gardens. Much of the National Trust's plant conservation work is coordinated from the Plant Conservation Centre in Devon (opposite), where rare or vulnerable trees from gardens and countryside properties are propagated and raised by specialist staff before being returned for planting. The centre also propagates native trees threatened with disease: junipers from the downlands of Dorset have been grown to re-establish populations hit by the pathogen *Phytophthora austrocedri*, and other species are grown to regenerate native woodland devastated by ash dieback.

Trees have never been under greater threat. At the same time, they have never been more important for the wellbeing of humankind. Around 30 per cent of the world's tree species are estimated to be in danger of extinction yet they are an essential element of both our cultural heritage and environmental stability. Planting and tending trees is an increasingly important aspect of the National Trust's work. Over the next few decades, millions of trees will be planted to create new and diverse treescapes. Among them will be the next generation of great trees that will reach maturity towards the turn of the 22nd century.

50
GREAT TREES

Silent witness

Some famous trees are not so extraordinary in their own right but happen to have been in the right place at the right time when something remarkable took place. That's the case with the battered old sycamore that stands on the village green at Tolpuddle in Dorset. Here, in 1834, six agricultural workers regularly met beneath the tree's branches to form the Friendly Society of Agricultural Labourers and protest against the meagre farm wages of the time. The six were tried and sentenced to transportation to Australia under the Unlawful Oaths Act, designed to prevent workers forming trade unions and challenging the Establishment. Following massive public demonstrations against their sentence, they were pardoned and returned to England.

The Tolpuddle Martyrs' act of bravery is considered a seminal moment in the formation of the Trade Union Movement and the establishment of workers' rights. This tree symbolises their courageous and quiet acts in the face of injustice.

The tree is estimated to be about 300 years old so it would have been quite mature even in 1834. The diameter of its trunk seems out of proportion to the small branches and modest height. That's because the tree has been

regularly pollarded to prevent it getting top-heavy and collapsing.

Although often considered a native species, sycamore was introduced from mainland Europe. How and when it got here is not known but it's now fully naturalised throughout the British Isles. Like all species of maples, sycamore has a type of winged fruit known as a samara. These helicopter-like structures are an evolutionary adaption to help distribute the seed widely.

Tolpuddle, Dorset · The Martyrs' Sycamore · *Acer pseudoplatanus* · *Family: Sapindaceae (soapberry)* · *Deciduous* · *Height: varies due to pollarding* · *Girth: 5.5m* · *Origin: mainland Europe and West Asia*

Opposite · Between 30,000 and 100,000 people attended a demonstration at Copenhagen Fields, London, on 21 April 1834 to protest against the sentences imposed on the Tolpuddle Martyrs. This engraving of 1834 by W. Summers was dedicated by the publisher, Isaiah Saunders, to Thomas Wakley MP, who campaigned on behalf of the Martyrs.

A tree with a price on its head

Sometimes introduced as the oldest resident of The Vyne, this veteran oak stands between the ornamental garden and the road. The story goes that in the early 1800s, the owner, William John Chute (1757–1824), was offered £100 for the tree by a prospecting merchant seeking timber for the shipyards. The offer was turned down but it was improved the following day to 100 guineas (£105, the equivalent of around £4,600 today). Chute is said to have remarked that any tree that increased in value by 5 per cent in one day was too valuable to lose, and the merchant was sent packing.

There are just two native species of oak in the British Isles: English or pedunculate oak (*Quercus robur*) and sessile oak (*Quercus petraea*). This tree is English oak, which can be distinguished from sessile (meaning stalkless) oak by the presence of stalks called peduncles that attach to the acorn cups. It is the most common oak in the lowlands and south of England, and the natural curves of its trunk and large limbs were used by shipwrights and builders to provide strong unjointed structures. This oak is estimated to be around 600 years old. Over the centuries it has survived storms, droughts, loss of limbs and the construction of a road alongside it. These disturbances have all left their marks in its

'body language' of buttresses, ridges and cavities. Unlike animals, trees grow throughout their lives and can respond to damage and disturbances, correcting any imbalance by growing new limbs and laying down extra wood tissue in the areas of stress. Humans have given this tree a bit of extra help by providing a prop to prevent it leaning further.

The Vyne, Hampshire · The Hundred Guinea Oak
· *Quercus robur* · *Family: Fagaceae (beech)* · *Deciduous*
· *Height: 22m*

Right · Plate I, 'Oak', from *The Spirit of the Woods* (1837) by Rebecca Hey, Anglesey Abbey, Cambridgeshire (NT 3101594).

Growing old with style

When famous landscape architect Lancelot 'Capability' Brown (1716–83) was planning his extravagant schemes for wealthy clients such as the 6th Earl of Coventry (1722–1809) at Croome Park, he had in mind the idealised landscapes portrayed in 17th-century art. Neo-classical painters such as Claude Lorrain (1600–82) depicted scenes that combined shady retreats, sweeping vistas, and tantalising glimpses of distant classical buildings or picturesque ruins (page 34). In the hands of exponents such as Brown, this combination of landscape qualities became known as the English Landscape Garden style. Stately trees were an essential element and Brown often chose cedar of Lebanon for its evergreen habit, distinctive layered branches and silhouette (pages 36–7). It's just as well that cedars are also long-lived, because trees like these provide a living link with that period of landscape history.

Interestingly, Lord Coventry bought his first cedar of Lebanon for Croome in 1748, three years before employing Brown to remodel the estate. Detailed accounts record that the first tree was eight feet tall and cost two guineas. Many more were purchased in the following years. This tree grows close to the Rotunda, built in around 1760 as part of Brown's grand

scheme, and is thought to have been planted shortly afterwards. The many other mature trees at Croome are all of a similar age and the National Trust has been pre-empting their eventual decline by planting young replacements.

There are just four species of cedar in the world. Cedar of Lebanon grows in mountainous areas of South-west Asia, including Syria and Lebanon. Its timber is highly prized for construction, joinery and furniture making, and the species now survives in a few fragmented areas of protected forest. Some of the recently planted trees at Croome have been grown from seed collected from wild trees on Mount Lebanon to support efforts to conserve this endangered conifer.

Croome, Worcestershire · Cedar of Lebanon · *Cedrus libani · Family: Pinaceae (pine) · Evergreen · Origin: South-west Asia · Introduced to UK: c.1645*

Opposite · The Father of Psyche Sacrificing at the Temple of Apollo (1662–3) by Claude Lorrain (1600–82), oil on canvas, 175.3 x 222.9cm, Anglesey Abbey, Cambridgeshire (NT 515656).

Right · Lancelot ('Capability') Brown (c.1770–5) after Sir Nathaniel Dance-Holland, RA (1735–1811), oil on canvas, 45.8 x 35.6cm, Wimpole, Cambridgeshire (NT 207914).

What's in a name?

This elder statesman encroaches onto one of Glendurgan's many paths, requiring admirers to give it right of way as they pass under its mighty limbs. It was planted in 1830 by Alfred Fox (1794–1874), who created the garden from the 1820s onwards, and its somewhat battered appearance is evidence of a life spent in the line of storms that sweep in from the sea. One such extreme weather event was recorded in 1929 by Edgar Thurston (1855–1935) in his publication *British and Foreign Trees and Shrubs in Cornwall* (1930).

The tulip tree gets its common name from the somewhat deceptive flowers, which resemble tulips. They appear in June and are borne high in the tree's crown, making them difficult to see with the naked eye. The leaves have an unusual and easily recognised three-lobed shape and turn bright yellow in autumn. The tulip tree was one of the first trees to be introduced to British gardens from eastern North America in the mid-17th century. The first known tree, planted in 1688, was collected by the famous botanist and head gardener to Charles I, John Tradescant the Younger (1608–62).

Common names are often misleading when it comes to understanding plant relationships.

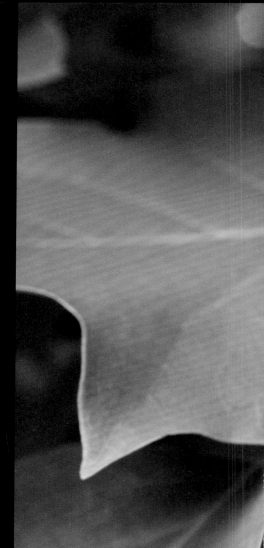

Tulip trees and garden tulips are not related botanically, despite the visual similarity of their flowers. This species is actually related to magnolias. The term 'tree' simply describes a large woody plant and says nothing about where it sits in the classification of plants. To add to the confusion, the wood from the tulip tree is often called yellow poplar despite the species being unrelated. It is highly versatile, with uses ranging from matchsticks to furniture, as well as mechanical parts for pianos and organs.

Glendurgan Garden, Cornwall · Tulip tree · *Liriodendron tulipifera* · Family: Magnoliaceae (magnolia) · Deciduous · Origin: eastern North America · Best seen in summer

Right · Plate 275, 'Liriodendron Tulipifera', from *The Botanical Magazine; or, Flower-garden Displayed*, vol. 7–8 (1794) by William Curtis, Anglesey Abbey, Cambridgeshire (NT 3238597).

N. 275

Pub. by W. Curtis, S.¹ Geo.⁵ Crescent. Sep. 1. 1794.

A tree with a view

Situated in the woods overlooking the idyllic Menai Straits, this magnificent old tree is reckoned to be the largest beech in the UK, with a girth of around 10 metres. Its main trunk rises only to about head height before dividing into a crown of massive main limbs. It appears to grow on an old wood bank and was probably pruned in this way to mark a boundary for management or ownership purposes. It acquired a more ornamental role during the heyday of the Plas Newydd estate, when the walking route through the woods in which it stands was created as a picturesque perambulation from the house and gardens.

This tree is extremely old by beech standards and there are areas of decay and deadwood in the trunk and limbs. Beech wood is not as durable as oak, and is more easily colonised by fungi, some of which produce intricate patterns called spalting. The black lines, called zone lines, are created by the fungi themselves where territories of competing colonies meet. Spalting is highly prized by furniture-makers and wood-turners.

Plas Newydd House and Garden, Anglesey · Ancient beech · *Fagus sylvatica* · *Family: Fagaceae (beech)* · *Deciduous* · *Best seen in autumn for fungi and leaf colour*

A tree with teeth

This elegant zelkova stretches its long limbs across the old ha-ha that separates the formal garden from the park at Tyntesfield and proves that not all great trees are tall. As well as having architectural quality, the tree has textured, flaking bark, which provides year-round interest, and the leaves turn glorious shades of bronze and red in autumn (overleaf). The 'serrata' part of the tree's Latin name comes from its coarsely toothed leaves.

Keaki, as this species is known in its native Japan, is often planted for ornament and shade in urban streets, and its versatile wood is used for everything from cutlery to carving and musical instruments. It was introduced to Britain in 1861 and would have been a botanical curiosity when the Gibbs family of Tyntesfield were designing the garden and planting it with newly introduced plants during the 1860s and 1870s. Its eventual size was unknown at that time, but this individual has grown to become one of the finest in the UK.

Zelkova is a small genus of trees closely related to elms and sometimes planted as an alternative following the devastation wrought by Dutch elm disease.

Tyntesfield, North Somerset · Japanese zelkova · *Zelkova serrata* · *Family: Ulmaceae (elm)* · *Deciduous* · *Origin: Japan, Korea, China and Taiwan* · *Introduced to UK: 1861* · *Best seen in summer and autumn*

Arboreal engineering

Douglas fir is a conifer from western North America, where it can grow to over 85 metres tall. It's not actually a true fir but more closely related to spruce and can be identified from its soft, flattened needles and pendulous cones. It inherits its name from the famous Scottish plant collector David Douglas (1799–1834), who introduced the species to the UK in 1827. It is a valuable timber tree and has been extensively planted in commercial plantations, including on the wider Cragside estate. The trees planted in the valley (right) have a more ornamental purpose, having been planted by Lord Armstrong (1810–1900) during the craze for big conifers in the 19th century. Armstrong was clearly very keen on such towering specimens for their landscape impact. He planted a number of other species in the pinetum (page 51), which could be viewed from the mansion across the valley.

In its species name, *Pseudotsuga menziesii*, Douglas fir acknowledges a second man: surgeon and explorer Archibald Menzies (1754–1842). Menzies was a celebrated botanist who served with the Royal Navy on the Vancouver Expedition that circumnavigated the globe between 1791 and 1795. He was responsible for collecting and introducing many plants to Britain, including the monkey puzzle. Naming plants to commemorate

people was part of the system of patronage during the period of colonial expansion and plant acquisition. Many plants were named after expedition sponsors as a reward for their financial support.

One of the defining features of a tree is height, and in Britain Douglas fir has few rivals. Evolution has favoured those that can elevate their foliage higher than surrounding competitors in the quest for sunlight. But height comes with a major challenge: raising water to such great elevation to supply thirsty leaves is no mean feat, and physicists have argued for centuries about how trees achieve this. We now know that a combination of negative pressure generated by evaporation from leaves and positive osmotic pressure from the roots forces water up continuous columns of specialist cells that form a vast and complex plumbing system. No doubt Lord Armstrong, a brilliant scientist, engineer and industrialist, would have been impressed.

Cragside, Northumberland · Douglas fir · *Pseudotsuga menziesii* · *Family: Pinaceae (pine)* · *Evergreen* · *Height: c.60m* · *Age: approx. 150 years*

Left · *Sir William George Armstrong, 1st Baron Armstrong of Cragside* (1878) by George Frederic Watts, RA (1817–1904), oil on canvas, 65.5 x 52.5cm, Cragside, Northumberland (NT 1230213).

The trees that just keep giving

Gnarly old hornbeams are a characteristic feature of the medieval hunting woodlands of Hatfield Forest. They have stood here for centuries with deer and cattle grazing around their trunks, taking advantage of the shade and shelter they provide. Their distinctive shape is evidence of pollarding, the traditional woodland management practice of regular lopping to harvest branches and foliage. Trees managed in this way are called pollards and often survive to a great age, despite their hollow trunks and distorted appearance.

An important characteristic shared by most of our native broadleaved trees is their ability to regrow spontaneously from cut stumps or limbs. This adaptation evolved to allow trees to respond to damage caused by browsing wild animals or storms. Humans have utilised this power of regeneration to meet their need for wood without the requirement for replanting. In the areas of Hatfield Forest grazed by cattle, pollards are lopped at around head height, just above browsing level. In ungrazed woodlands, trees are lopped at ground level (coppiced). The harvested foliage would have been used as fodder for cattle or deer.

Hornbeam gets its name from the qualities of its wood: horn meaning hard and beam being the Old English word for tree. Its strength and resistance to abrasion made it ideal for a range of specialist applications including agricultural implements, and cogwheels and cams in windmills and other machinery. Charcoal made from its wood burns at very high temperatures and was used for smelting iron before coke became more commonly used.

Hornbeam flowers (right) are arranged in hanging catkins that appear in April or May.

Hatfield Forest National Nature Reserve, Essex
· Pollarded hornbeams · *Carpinus betulus* · *Family: Betulaceae (birch)* · *Deciduous*

Mr Lucombe's happy accident

Many of the mature trees at Dyffryn are a legacy of the entrepreneur and plant-lover Reginald Cory (1871–1934). The horticultural origins of this impressive oak lie over a century earlier. In around 1762, William Lucombe (1696–1794), owner of a nursery near Exeter, noticed that some seedlings grown from the acorns of a Turkey oak showed characteristics of cork oak instead. These included a tendency to retain their leaves through winter and a moderately corky bark. It became clear that pollen from a nearby cork oak tree had fertilised the flowers of the Turkey oak and the seedlings were hybrids (*Quercus x hispanica*). Lucombe took advantage of this serendipity and propagated more of these unusual trees for his clients.

The parent species of *Q. x hispanica* grow together in southern Europe and hybrids occur naturally. The offspring are intermediate in habit between evergreen cork oak and deciduous Turkey oak. The leaves are usually retained until around the New Year with only a short period before they are replaced by new ones, a habit that is known as semi-deciduous.

Dyffryn Gardens, Vale of Glamorgan · The Lucombe Oak · *Quercus x hispanica 'Lucombeana'* · Family: Fagaceae (beech) · Semi-deciduous

Tough townie

Few trees are more characteristic of city streets and parks than the London plane. Its origins are also intimately bound up with human activity: the parent species of this hybrid grow naturally in North America and southern Europe, but it wasn't until the 17th century and the introduction of plants from north-eastern USA that the two species were grown together in European gardens, allowing them to interbreed. This fortuitous event produced vigorous offspring with a remarkable ability to survive the rough-and-tumble of urban life, especially polluted air and repeated severe pruning. These qualities, and the tree's magnificent stature, made it a popular choice with 18th- and 19th-century town planners all over Europe. It also became a popular tree for planting in large gardens and parks such as Mottisfont. The tree shown here is the largest of many impressive London plane trees in the garden, no doubt enjoying the plentiful water supply from the nearby stream.

London plane is easily identified by its flaking, camouflage-patterned bark (overleaf). The shape of the maple-like leaves is intermediate between the deep lobes of the Oriental plane (*Platanus orientalis*) and the shallower lobes of the American sycamore (*Platanus occidentalis*), these being the two parent species.

Mottisfont, Hampshire · London plane · *Platanus x hispanica* · *Family: Platanaceae (plane)* · *Deciduous* · *Height: c.30m · Girth: 8m*

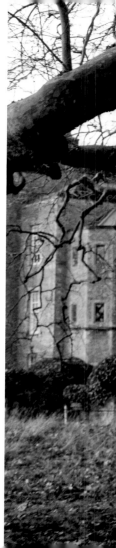

Weeping beauty

This fountain of a tree sits squarely in the middle of the lawn at Seaton Delaval Hall. Some of the limbs of this weeping ash have been propped to prevent them collapsing, adding to its venerable charm. Individual pendulous ash trees occur every now and again in nature as chance variants to the usual form. Through genetic mutation they lack the hormone-guided instinct to grow towards the light, and instead follow gravitational force downwards. Few would survive if it weren't for the appeal they have to novelty-seeking gardeners. They are propagated by grafting the pendulous shoots onto normally shaped trunks to create two trees in one. Many other novel characteristics, such as variegated or unusually shaped leaves, are perpetuated in a similar way. Trees showing these variations are known as 'sports'.

The British Isles have just one native species of ash. Its wood is strong and flexible and was traditionally used for a variety of mechanically demanding purposes from tool handles to hockey sticks and farm implements.

In recent years a deadly fungal pathogen known as ash dieback has spread rapidly across Europe, killing millions of ash trees. The disease occurs naturally in eastern Asia, where it coexists with the various species of ash indigenous to the region. It is especially prevalent in more densely spaced woodland trees and, with luck, this individual tree will not succumb.

In November 2021, as this book was being prepared, Storm Arwen resulted in the loss of most of the tree's crown. The storm's gale-force winds brought down large numbers of trees across the north of England and Wales, including some of the most exceptional specimens in the National Trust's care, demonstrating the growing risk posed by extreme weather events driven by climate change.

Seaton Delaval Hall, Northumberland · Weeping ash · *Fraxinus excelsior 'Pendula' · Family: Oliaceae (olive) · Deciduous · Age: approx. 300 years · Origin: Europe and the Caucasus*

A real corker

This eye-catching oak is believed to have been planted in the late 18th century when the Georgian landscape of Osterley Park was being developed. The trees chosen to help shape the landscape had to provide living structure to complement the building in scale and impressive appearance. Novelty was also a desirable quality and this oak was one of the first of its kind to be planted in England. It is a county champion and one of the 'Great Trees of London', a list created after the devastating Great Storm of 1987.

Bark is hugely variable, reflecting its many functions in helping trees adapt to the range of environments in which they live. Protection from extremes of temperature, dehydration and attack from insect pests and disease are all important functions. Some trees produce a thick outer layer of bark, known as cork, impregnated with a waxy substance called suberin. Cork has remarkable qualities of flexibility, insulation and impermeability to water and gases, all necessary for surviving life in the hot, dry woodlands of southern Europe and North Africa. These attributes are also ideal for a range of industrial and domestic applications, not least the use of corks for sealing wine bottles, although increasingly these are being replaced with metal screwtops and plastic stoppers.

Cork trees are first harvested at about 25 years of age and then every nine years or so to give them a chance to regrow a new layer of bark. Great skill is needed to harvest the outer bark without damaging the living inner layers and killing the tree. Cork oak forests are valuable habitats for wildlife and the reduction in demand for bottle corks is threatening their continued management and conservation.

Osterley Park and House, Middlesex · Cork oak ·
*Quercus suber · Family: Fagaceae (beech) · Evergreen ·
Origin: southern Europe and North Africa*

Sisterhood

When garden designers want to create formal structure and dramatic effect, they often turn to Irish yew. This variant (or cultivar) of our native tree has a more upright stance and tighter branch structure than the wild form. These characteristics and its evergreen habit make it perfect for pruning into a variety of shapes, such as these curvy columns in the garden at Erddig. The yew walk was replanted by the National Trust as part of a restoration of the original 18th-century formal garden. The trees are regularly trimmed to maintain their precise and identical shapes. This may be done by skilled eye or using a metal or wooden frame to maintain symmetry.

All these trees and the millions of other Irish yews grown in gardens all over the world originate from just one tree growing at the National Trust's garden at Florence Court in County Fermanagh, Northern Ireland.

The original Irish yew was found as a young sapling growing on Cuilcagh Mountain in 1765 by local farmer George Willis. Attracted by the tree's unusual vertical branching or 'fastigiate' form, Willis dug it up and gave it to nearby Florence Court, where it has grown by the Claddagh River ever since. The tree turned out to be a female and is still going strong at over 250 years old, although she has lost some of

her distinctive shape. To replicate the unusual form, her countless offspring are propagated asexually through cuttings. Every tree bearing the name 'Fastigiata' is therefore a female and genetically identical to the original tree. Trees grown from seed collected from Irish yews will have been fertilised by a non-fastigiate male tree and would not exhibit the desired shape.

Erddig, Wrexham · Irish yews · *Taxus baccata 'Fastigiata'* · *Family: Taxaceae (yew)* · *Evergreen*

Left · Plate XIV, 'Yew', from *The Spirit of the Woods* (1837) by Rebecca Hey, Anglesey Abbey, Cambridgeshire (NT 3101594).

Opposite · Yew wood has a beautiful grain and can be steam-bent to produce the curved elements of furniture such as Windsor chairs like this one at Nunnington Hall, North Yorkshire (NT 980141.1).

Arboreal bling

Monkey puzzle is a bit of a Marmite tree: you either love it or you hate it. Perhaps that's down to its peculiar appearance, which can seem out of place in our historic landscapes. This tree stands as bold as brass close to the Neo-Palladian house at Calke, a relic of an age when it was de rigueur to plant unusual trees as a statement of wealth and status. Its somewhat untidy look seems to complement Calke's 'un-stately home' philosophy, reminding us that trees and other plants go in and out of fashion too.

Monkey puzzle became a horticultural hit in the Victorian period and is said to have gained its name when barrister and socialite Charles Austin (1799–1874) commented that to climb its sharp branches (overleaf) would puzzle even a monkey. Its timber is strong and resistant to decay and much sought after for building bridges, piers and ships. Its value has led to over-exploitation in the South American forests where it originates, and it is now classified 'endangered' by the International Union for the Conservation of Nature.

Calke Abbey, Derbyshire · Monkey puzzle · *Araucaria araucana* · Family: *Araucariaceae* · Evergreen · Origin: *Chile and Argentina* · Introduced to UK: 1795

Magnificent maidenhair

Antony House is a mecca for tree-lovers. Among its many great specimens is this magnificent maidenhair tree, which would, no doubt, have been a highly prized addition to the tree collection of Antony's former owner, Sir John Pole-Carew (1902–93). In its native China the maidenhair tree is considered sacred and is traditionally grown close to Buddhist temples. It is thought to be extinct in the wild but is planted as an urban street tree all over the world. Visually, it comes into its own in autumn, when its leaves turn a bright butter-yellow.

By and large, trees can be divided into broadleaves and conifers. Botanists use the terms angiosperm (enclosed seed) and gymnosperm (naked seed) respectively. Looking at the fern-like leaves of the maidenhair, you'd expect it to be a broadleaved tree. In fact, it is the only surviving species of an ancient family of trees related to conifers that grew in many areas of the world about 190 million years ago.

Antony, Cornwall · Maidenhair tree · *Ginkgo biloba* · *Family: Ginkgoaceae* · *Deciduous* · *Origin: China* · *Introduced to UK: 1754* · *Best seen in summer and autumn*

Right · Plate 168, 'Salisburia adiantifolia', from *Dendrologia Britannica* (1825) by P.W. Watson, Anglesey Abbey, Cambridgeshire (NT 3124740).

Pl.168.

Blooming refined

Hidcote is a garden of delicate beauty and this hill cherry perfectly complements its intimate scale and artistic spirit of place. Its bountiful white blossom arrives in mid-to-late April at about the same time as the bronzy young leaves. No wonder it is one of the best-loved trees of Japan, providing inspiration to poets and artists for centuries.

Japan is blessed with a remarkable diversity of indigenous tree flora, which includes several wild cherries, known collectively as *yama zakura*. Hill cherry is one of these wild species and it has provided the basis for the country's long tradition of hybridising and selection to produce ornamental garden varieties of great refinement. There are over 200 of these 'village cherries', or *sato zakura*. Over the centuries of breeding, their precise parentage has been forgotten, so rather than having complex botanical descriptions, they are given more evocative names such as Kiku Zakura (chrysanthemum-flowered cherry), Shizuka (fragrant cloud) and Tai Haku (great white).

Hanami is the Japanese tradition of observing and enjoying the transient beauty of cherry blossom (overleaf). In recent years the National Trust has introduced a British equivalent: Blossom Watch. If you're lucky enough to

catch this tree in bloom, please share your experience with us at #blossomwatch.

Britain has its own native cherries that provide a wild *hanami* in our hedgerows and woodlands. Blackthorn, or sloe, is the first to bloom in March, followed in April by the common wild cherry and the less frequent bird cherry. In May the hedgerows light up with the blossom of hawthorn.

Hidcote, Gloucestershire · Japanese hill cherry · *Prunus jamasakura · Family: Rosaceae (rose) · Deciduous · Origin: Japan, Korea and Taiwan · Introduced to UK: c.1914 · Best seen in spring*

The trees that built the West

The high rainfall of the Lake District makes it a good place for fast-growing conifers. The Tree Trail at High Close features several species, including this fabulous coast redwood. At around 40 metres, this tree is about a third of the height of the world's tallest tree, a 116-metre coast redwood growing in Redwood National Park in California. It is the iconic species of the Pacific Northwest coastal forests of the USA and, until the mid-19th century when commercial logging began, redwood forests covered nearly two million acres. Its timber has a natural resistance to decay and was favoured for railroad ties and trestle bridges. After many decades of uncontrolled exploitation, campaigning by pioneering conservationists such as John Muir (1838–1914) led to the establishment of reserves to protect it.

The thick, fibrous bark insulates the living inner bark from the natural fires that sweep through the coastal forests. The botanical name honours the Native American scholar Sequoyah (c.1775–1843), who is credited with developing a written form of the Cherokee language.

High Close Estate, Cumbria · Coast redwood · *Sequoia sempervirens* · *Family: Cupressaceae (cypress)* · *Evergreen* · *Origin: USA (California and Oregon)* · *Introduced to UK: 1843*

Reclining Roman

Living among the rarities and botanical VIPs of Bodnant's prestigious plant collection is this more down-to-earth sweet chestnut tree, better known for its impressive structure than any distinguished horticultural pedigree. It lives on the Top Lawn, where its accommodating low limbs provide welcome natural seating for weary visitors and entry-level challenge for novice tree-climbers. It was probably planted as a parkland tree well over 200 years ago, during Bodnant's Georgian period. Since losing its top in a storm many decades ago the tree has adopted a more sideways growth habit, with an elbow resting on the lawn for support.

Sweet chestnut was long thought to have been introduced to Britain by the Romans. However, in recent years scientists and historians have questioned this belief, with some arguing that it is actually a native species. Others favour a much later date of introduction, around the 7th century, pointing towards the lack of written references or physical evidence of its presence before then.

Whatever the truth, sweet chestnut has become an 'honorary native' and a common tree in woodlands, parks and gardens. Its nutritious nuts (overleaf) would certainly have been a welcome addition to the diet of early Britons,

CASTANEA *sativa* C.B.P.

and they have become a regular ingredient in our Christmas celebrations.

The timber of sweet chestnut is strong and durable and is often used in construction for beams and other load-bearing applications. It is easily split and small-dimension wood is widely used for posts and cleft fencing.

Bodnant Garden, Conwy · Sweet chestnut · *Castanea sativa* · Family: Fagaceae (beech) · Deciduous · Origin: southern Europe, North Africa, Asia Minor · *Best seen in autumn for nuts*

Left · Plate LXXXIV, 'Castanea sativa', from *Figures of the Most Beautiful, Useful, and Uncommon Plants* (1760) by Philip Miller, Anglesey Abbey, Cambridgeshire (NT 3051104).

Time-traveller

This old sycamore tree looks so settled in its hollow (known as 'Sycamore Gap') that it's easy to assume it has been here for as long as the Roman wall beside it. In fact, it's thought to be the last survivor of a larger group of sycamores planted here just a few hundred years ago. It has now become one of Hadrian's Wall's best-known landmarks, featuring in thousands of walkers' holiday pictures and selfies. In 2016 it was awarded the honour of being named England's Tree of the Year by the Woodland Trust. It's a movie star, too, having appeared in the 1991 film *Robin Hood: Prince of Thieves* alongside Kevin Costner. For some strange reason Robin passed this way between the White Cliffs of Dover and Nottingham Castle.

Sycamore is thought to have been introduced to Britain in the 15th century, 100 years or so after Robin Hood was robbing from the rich in the 13th or 14th century. Trees often present such problems of chronological inconsistency for film and television producers. Impossibly old cedar trees are often seen in Georgian period dramas and American conifers introduced in the 1850s show up in English medieval hunting scenes.

Hadrian's Wall and Housesteads Fort, Northumberland
• Sycamore • *Acer pseudoplatanus* • *Family: Sapindaceae (soapberry)* • *Deciduous* • *Origin: Europe (not British Isles) and West Asia*

Distinguished scholar

On an autumn day you can just imagine the young physicist Isaac Newton (1642–1727) sitting under this apple tree contemplating the fundamental forces of the universe. Woolsthorpe Manor was Newton's birthplace and family home and in 1665 he sought refuge here from plague-hit Cambridge to work on his scientific theories. It is said that the falling of an apple from this tree helped him to formulate his theory of gravity. Whether the apple actually fell on his head is an embellishment to the story that cannot be confirmed.

The tree's gravitational story continued when, in 2015, seeds collected from it were sent to the International Space Station. On their return, they were propagated and grown at various locations, including one at Woolsthorpe, planted by astronaut Tim Peake. Six months in zero gravity didn't seem to affect their growth and no doubt their apples will still fall to Earth.

Flower of Kent is one of thousands of traditional apple varieties, many of which have fallen out of favour as they are replaced by new ones with better flavour, texture or keeping qualities. Unfortunately, this variety has an unpleasant mealy texture and poor flavour and might have disappeared if it weren't for its distinguished backstory.

Despite its familiarity in our diets and culture, the domesticated apple is not a native species. Like many 'modern' food plants, it originates from wild ancestors, in this case a crab apple, *Malus sieversii*, from the mountains of Central Asia. Its long history of domestication began over 4,000 years ago and it probably spread westwards with nomadic people, perhaps in the dung of their horses. Through a gradual process of hybridisation with local crab apples and human selection, the large, flavoursome fruits we know today developed. *M. sieversii* is now stored in seed banks to conserve the genetic origins of this important food resource.

Like many other historical plant varieties, Flower of Kent has been preserved for posterity through propagation by the National Trust's Plant Conservation Centre in Devon. The descendants of this tree now grow at other gardens to provide security against disease or other losses.

Woolsthorpe Manor, Lincolnshire · Isaac Newton's Apple Tree · *Apple (Malus domestica 'Flower of Kent')* · *Family: Rosaceae (rose)* · *Deciduous* · *Best seen in spring and autumn*

Opposite · The frontispiece and title page of the 1726 edition of Sir Isaac Newton's *Philosophiæ Naturalis Principia Mathematica* (first published in 1687), Woolsthorpe Manor, Lincolnshire (NT 3055615).

ISAACUS NEWTON EQ. AUR. ÆT. 83.

PHILOSOPHIÆ

NATURALIS

PRINCIPIA

MATHEMATICA.

AUCTORE

ISAACO NEWTONO, Eq. Aur.

Editio tertia aucta & emendata.

Apud Guil. & Joh. Innys, Regiæ Societatis typographos.
MDCCXXVI.

Tree calendar

This magnificent beech avenue is one of the great landmarks of Dorset. It was planted in 1835 by Kingston Lacy's owner, William John Bankes (1786–1855), as an extravagant memorial to his mother, Frances. There were 365 trees planted on one side of the road to represent each day of the year, and 366 on the other side for a leap year. At the time, the road was a turnpike that provided revenue for the estate. It is now the B3082, a free 2½-mile drive-through attraction for travellers between Wimborne and Blandford, especially popular in autumn when it provides a colour sensation.

Avenues are intended to present an appearance of regularity, with trees of equal age and stature providing uniformity. This poses particular challenges to managers of mature avenues where severe weather and disease threaten to disturb well-laid plans and create a more chaotic appearance. As some trees decline before others, replanting inevitably leads to a more gap-toothed appearance.

Beech is not as long-lived as oak and many of the trees in the avenue, now over 180 years old, are showing signs of decay and disease. In a woodland situation this would not be a great problem but alongside a busy road the trees need constant monitoring and, where

necessary, removal and replacement. The National Trust has already had to replace many of them, and young trees can be seen in some sections. Hornbeam has been chosen to replace beech as it provides similar autumn colour but is considered more resilient to our changing climate.

Kingston Lacy, Dorset · Beech Avenue · *Fagus sylvatica* · *Family: Fagaceae (beech)* · *Deciduous* · *Best seen in autumn for leaf colour*

Left · Plate IV, 'Beech', from *The Spirit of the Woods* (1837) by Rebecca Hey, Anglesey Abbey, Cambridgeshire (NT 3101594).

National champion

Every now and again a tree becomes so well known for its extraordinary size or beauty that it is given a name all of its own. That's the case with the famous Montezuma pine of Sheffield Park, a national champion at over 18 metres in height. It was planted in 1910 by Arthur Gilstrap Soames (1854–1934), the brewing magnate who purchased Sheffield Park in 1909. Soames was a knowledgeable horticulturalist and he was responsible for creating much of the colourful treescape we see at Sheffield Park today.

Montezuma pine grows wild in the mountains of Mexico and Central America but it's quite a rare sight in this country. This specimen shows the domed crown of greyish-green foliage typical of the species. Unlike our native Scots pine, the needles are held in clusters of five (rather than two) and are much longer. In its native forests, the species can reach over 30 metres and it is grown in commercial plantations for construction timber. It yields a wealth of other useful products: resin from the pulp wood is used to extract vanillin, a substitute for vanilla.

Sheffield Park and Garden, East Sussex · Montezuma pine · *Pinus montezumae 'Sheffield Park'* · *Family: Pinaceae (pine)* · *Evergreen* · *Height: 18m+* · *Girth: 3.5m* · *Origin: Mexico, Guatemala and Nicaragua (indigenous name: ocote)* · *Introduced to UK: 1839*

Love it or hate it

Some trees get a bad reputation through no fault of their own. Sitka spruce is much favoured by foresters but loathed in equal measure by conservationists for being the tree that thrives in industrial plantations in Britain's uplands. The wet, mild climate of western Britain is a good match for Sitka's native Pacific Northwest, and it grows at a prodigious rate. The product is straight-grained timber suited to a range of uses including construction and paper production. Its flexibility, high strength-to-weight ratio and good acoustic qualities have also been utilised in a range of more demanding products including aircraft frames and musical instruments such as guitars and violins.

Despite its reputation for despoiling our upland landscapes, Sitka spruce is a beautiful tree when grown in a more naturalistic way. Aira Force is often referred to as a woodland garden, a form of designed landscape that became fashionable during the 19th century. The style drew on the Victorian taste for displaying plants and animals gathered from all over the world, and Aira Force provided a fitting natural gallery. During the 1840s, the Howard Family of Greystoke Castle planted this arboretum of exotic species to 'improve' the already dramatic Lakeland landscape.

With only around 13 per cent tree cover, the UK is one of the least forested countries in Europe. Many of our upland forests where Sitka spruce grows were originally planted following the two world wars to provide a strategic reserve of timber. During the wars, access to our traditional timber supply from North America was threatened by the Atlantic U-boat blockades, so the nation had to turn to felling trees and woodland to make pit props for coal mining and to meet other essential needs. The Forestry Commission was established to oversee the work of replanting, favouring fast-growing conifers over native species. There is now a new impetus to increase forest cover to tackle climate change and increase biodiversity.

Aira Force, Cumbria · Sitka spruce · *Picea sitchensis* · *Family: Pinaceae (pine)* · *Evergreen* · *Origin: North America (Pacific coast, California to Alaska)*

Leaf peeping

Winkworth Arboretum is renowned for its glorious autumn colour and it is no surprise that its creator, Dr Wilfrid Fox (1875–1962), was a fan of Japanese maples. Individual specimens are impressive enough but these modestly sized trees really pack a punch when planted in groups (overleaf). The display varies in quality and timing from year to year depending on weather conditions but each tree in the group contributes subtly different shades of red and orange to the overall effect.

In Japan, Japanese maple is the tree most closely associated with *momijigari*: the tradition of celebrating autumn through the colouring of leaves. In North America 'leaf peeping' has become a popular pastime with many fans taking autumn breaks to New England and other colour hotspots. In the UK, too, the popularity of getting out in the autumn to enjoy the vibrant colours has grown rapidly and the National Trust provides regular updates on the state of the leaves and the best gardens to visit.

The autumn colouring of deciduous plants is a massive natural phenomenon that occurs right across the temperate northern regions of the world. Over a period of several weeks a band of colour passes north to south from the Arctic to the warm Mediterranean climates, where the colour fizzles out as evergreen plants prevail.

Winkworth Arboretum, Surrey · Japanese maples · *Acer palmatum* · *Family: Sapindaceae (maple)* · *Deciduous* · *Origin: Japan, China, Korea and Taiwan* · *Introduced to UK: 1820*

Welsh castle

The landscape of Dinefwr Park (overleaf) is a haven for veteran oak trees and the wildlife they support. There are around 300 ancient oaks (more than 400 years old) here and the Castle Oak, at around 800, is the grandest and oldest of them all. It provides a living link to the medieval ancestry of the park, and the centuries have left their mark in its diverse morphology of bulges, cavities and deadwood. Add to this the cool, humid climate of Wales and the result is one of the richest assemblages of old-growth lichen and bryophyte communities in the UK. Over 160 lichens have been recorded living on the various surfaces and microclimates provided by the trees. Most importantly, the trees of Dinefwr Park have provided continuity through a sequence of landscape changes as the politics, economics and wildlife of Wales have shifted around them.

The roving historian and archdeacon Gerallt Cymro (Gerald of Wales, c.1146–c.1223) (left) visited Dinefwr in 1194, shortly after the castle was built, and commented that 'it is well protected by its site and surrounded by woods'.

Left · Gerald of Wales depicted in a stained-glass window of 1915 by C.E. Kempe & Co Ltd in the Church of St James, Manorbier, Pembrokeshire.

Gerald travelled widely in his ecclesiastical duties and his written accounts of the people, landscapes and wildlife of Wales provide us with unique and valuable historical information. We know, for example, that beavers and wild pigs were still common but there is no account of wolves, which became extinct around that time.

Several centuries and wars later the woodland took on a more genteel function within a landscaped parkland. Another observer, the writer Benjamin Heath Malkin (1769–1842), gave a rather opinionated review of Lord Dynevor's approach to management:

There is a great deal of old timber, which might be cut down without at all detracting from the sylvan character of the scene; and the young plantations which are thriving fast, would more than supply the loss.

Dinefwr Park is now a National Nature Reserve.

Dinefwr, Carmarthenshire · The Castle Oak · *Quercus robur · Family: Fagaceae (beech) · Deciduous*

Botanical booty

An exploration of the garden at Biddulph is like a botanical world tour. When you reach China, you'll encounter this beautiful conifer. At over 150 years old, it's a lot older than it looks and it was one of the original trees collected from the wild and transported to Britain by the renowned plant collector Robert Fortune (1812–80). Golden larch shares a name and its deciduous habit with larch, but this is a very different species, more closely related to cedar. The golden epithet comes from the gorgeous tones of its autumn foliage.

James Bateman (1811–97) lavished his inherited wealth on creating the garden at Biddulph and filling it with irresistible plants. This was an era when botanical treasures were plundered from all over the world, often against the will of national authorities. Robert Fortune disguised himself as a Chinese person to evade attention while collecting plants for his clients. Today, such collection and use of genetic resources is regulated by international agreements.

Biddulph Grange Garden, Staffordshire · Fortune's Golden Larch · *Pseudolarix amabilis* · *Family: Pinaceae (pine)* · *Deciduous* · *Origin: eastern China* · *Introduced to UK: 1852* · *Best seen from May to October*

Function and beauty

One of the most beautiful but elusive sights in the garden at Emmetts is the brief flowering of the handkerchief trees. For just two or three weeks in May the branches become festooned with the delicate flower bracts (overleaf), which resemble freshly laundered handkerchiefs. The species inherits its generic name from the French missionary and natural historian Father Armand David (1826–1900), who studied and recorded the plants and animals of China in the late 19th century (he is thought to have been the first European to observe the giant panda).

The white bracts of the handkerchief tree have an aesthetic appeal to human admirers but a much more practical purpose for the tree. In fact, they are multi-functional miracles of plant evolution: each flower has a pair of bracts that, as they emerge, change from green to white over a few days. Strictly speaking, they are not part of the flower at all but leaf-like structures that form an umbrella-like whorl, known as an involucre, around the small and inconspicuous flowers within. As they change colour, they lose their photosynthetic function and increase in their UV light absorbance, making them highly visible to pollinating bees. The umbrella structure also acts as a rain shelter to protect the vulnerable pollen.

When descriptions of this beautiful tree first reached Europe in the late 19th century, commercial nurseries were keen to acquire it for sale to their customers. One such firm was Veitch Nurseries, who dispatched young botanist Ernest Henry Wilson (1876–1930) to China to collect its seed. In his written account of the highs and lows of his search, Wilson recalls:

We sallied forth, I in the highest of spirits. After walking about two miles we came to a house rather new in appearance. Nearby was the stump of Henry's Davidia. The tree had been cut down a year before and the trunk and branches formed the beams and posts of the house! I did not sleep during the night of April 25, 1900.

On May 19th, when collecting near the hamlet of Ta-wan, distant some five days southwest of Ichang, I suddenly happened upon a Davidia tree in full flower!

Emmetts Garden, Kent · Handkerchief tree · *Davidia involucrata* · Family: Nyssaceae (sour gum) · Deciduous · Origin: China · Introduced to UK: 1904 · Best seen in May

Shabby chic

Scots pine is Britain's only native pine and one of only three native conifers. It has a more interesting shape than many pines, with attractive rusty-orange young bark on the upper trunk and branches.

Leading landscape designer Humphry Repton (1752–1818) was commissioned by the new owners, Abbot Upcher (1785–1819) and his wife Charlotte (1790–1857), to produce a plan for Sheringham Park in 1812. The plan was presented as one of his famous Red Books, written in his own hand and illustrated with watercolour sketches. In the late 18th century the landscape style championed by Lancelot 'Capability' Brown (1716–83) was falling out of favour. A new style called Picturesque was gaining popularity, and savvy advisers such as Repton were quick to jump ship and adopt the new vogue. It favoured a more relaxed approach, with woody plants chosen for their more naturalistic appearance. Scots pine was a particular favourite.

Sheringham Park, Norfolk · Scots pine · *Pinus sylvestris* ·
Family: Pinaceae (pine) · *Evergreen*

Right · Plate 207, 'Pinus sylvestris', from *A Supplement to Medical Botany* (1794) by William Woodville, Anglesey Abbey, Cambridgeshire (NT 3124738).

207

Pinus sylvestris

Published by W. Woodville, June 1, 1793.

Botanical sweetshop

A tight cluster of katsura trees (opposite) provides one of the most memorable experiences of autumn at Sizergh. The species is sometimes referred to as 'candyfloss tree', and if you walk past in autumn as the leaves begin to turn you may get a heady waft of the burnt-sugar scent that explains why. The foliage of katsura also has a striking visual beauty; the heart-shaped leaves are arranged in opposite pairs along the branches, giving them a chain-like appearance. In autumn they turn a variety of shades of yellow and smoky pink (overleaf).

Trees exhibit a variety of flowering habits: some, such as apples, are hermaphrodites, with flowers that include both male and female parts. Others have separate male and female flowers on the same plant. Oaks and birches are examples of this 'monoecious' habit. This species is different again: it is 'dioecious', meaning that each tree has either male (left) or female flowers but never both. The cluster of katsuras growing in this part of the garden at Sizergh includes trees of both sexes.

Sizergh, Cumbria · Katsura · *Cercidiphyllum japonicum* · *Family: Cercidiphyllaceae · Deciduous · Origin: Japan · Introduced to UK: 1881*

Conker champion

Horse chestnut is an introduced tree that has settled comfortably into the British landscape and is now accepted as an honourable native. This individual stands in the Hughenden parkland, and with a girth of over 7 metres has been awarded the status of champion tree. It almost certainly predates the many trees planted by Benjamin Disraeli (1804–81) and his wife Mary Anne (1792–1872), who occupied the property in the 19th century. By midsummer the leaves of this and other horse chestnuts often become brown and disfigured due to damage by the horse chestnut leaf-miner moth. But despite this, and its great age, the tree still produces an abundance of conkers every year (overleaf).

The designation of champion tree is awarded by the Tree Register of the British Isles (TROBI). Champions are the tallest or 'fattest' of their species at a national or county level. This tree is a national champion, with the broadest girth in the UK. Many National Trust gardens and parks are homes to champion trees.

Measuring trees is carried out by foresters and dendrologists for a variety of purposes. As well as judging whether a tree is a champion, it can be used to estimate the volume of timber or as a guide to age. Girth or diameter is measured at chest level (1.5 metres). Height

is more complicated and traditionally relied on measuring angles and using trigonometric calculations. Nowadays, digital instruments do the hard work and the maths.

The game of conkers is thought to have developed from an earlier one, played with hazelnuts and snail shells and popular before the horse chestnut was introduced to Britain. The first recorded use of conkers wasn't until 1848, on the Isle of Wight. Since 1965 the World Conker Championships have been held on the second Sunday in October in Northamptonshire.

Hughenden, Buckinghamshire · Horse chestnut ·
Aesculus hippocastanum · *Family: Sapindaceae (soapberry)*
· *Deciduous* · *Girth: 7.3m* · *Origin: Greece and Albania* ·
Introduced to UK: early 17th century · *Best seen in*
autumn for conkers

Eccentric relative

From a distance this tree could easily be overlooked as just another beautiful beech tree in the park at Kedleston. But closer examination of this arboricultural curiosity reveals that the leaves are not at all like normal beech, but have a lobed, fern-like shape (overleaf). The tree doesn't grow as tall as a regular beech but forms a wide, spreading crown and certainly competes when it comes to autumn leaf colour, with a glorious display of gold and bronze.

Other common trees also have unusual varieties, including cut-leaved silver birch and common alder. Over time, variants like this often return to the typical form, a process known as reversion. Fortunately, this tree is showing no sign of that and retains a full crown of fern-leaved foliage.

Leaf shape is a good way to identify trees and a rich vocabulary of terms is used to describe different shapes and edge details (page 195). The overall shape of a normal beech leaf is described as ovate (egg-shaped) with an entire margin. The fern-leaved beech, by contrast, has leaves with deeply cut lobes. Not far from this beech you'll find trees with a wide variety of other leaf shapes including some with serrated or wavy (undulate) margins.

Kedleston Hall, Derbyshire · Fern-leaved beech · *Fagus sylvatica 'Aspleniifolia' · Family: Fagaceae (beech) · Deciduous · Best seen in summer or autumn*

Botanical star

Lanhydrock is well known for its spring display of flowering trees and shrubs. The magnolias are the stars of the show and this tree is a prima donna whose brilliant white flowers demand attention in early spring. It was planted in 1974 and awarded the name Albatross by the International Magnolia Society to indicate its distinctive characteristics.

Many of the garden's mature magnolias were planted in the mid-20th century by Francis Gerald Agar-Robartes, 7th Viscount Clifden (1883–1966), who owned Lanhydrock and recognised the suitability of its mild climate and sheltered position. Since the 1960s the National Trust has planted many more of these wonderful trees, ranging in colour from dark purple to pure white.

There are over 200 species of magnolias indigenous to Asia, and to North and South America. It is a primitive group of plants that fossil evidence shows existed over 100 million years ago. The trees are thought to have evolved to be pollinated by beetles, abundant during the Cretaceous Period.

Lanhydrock, Cornwall · Magnolia 'Albatross' · *Family: Magnoliaceae (magnolia) · Deciduous · Origin: Garden hybrid · Best seen in early spring*

Fine dining

Mulberry trees have a habit of gaining picturesque character as they grow old and this one is no exception. Its sprawling appearance came about in 2000, when it was blown over in high winds. Undeterred, it has continued to thrive and still produces a fine crop of berries every year despite its horizontal trunk.

Since medieval times mulberries have been grown in monasteries and gardens for their fruit (pages 140–1). In Elizabethan times, they became quite a status symbol, with trees grown to provide an impressive treat at banquets. It's tempting to imagine this tree growing in the garden during Chastleton's Jacobean heyday. However, despite its ancient appearance, it probably dates back to 1837, when records indicate that a mulberry tree was planted in the garden.

There's some uncertainty about the arrival of the mulberry in Britain but the seeds have been found in excavated Roman settlements close to the Thames in London. The fruit is highly perishable so these must have been grown nearby.

Mulberry leaves are the sole food of silkworms, so to produce silk you must first grow mulberry trees. In 1607 King James I (1566–1625), jealous of the lucrative Italian

and French silk industries, ordered the nobility to plant mulberries to establish a counterpart industry in England. The venture failed, perhaps because black mulberry was planted rather than white (*Morus alba*), which produces finer silk. Despite this false start, a thriving silk industry developed by the 18th century using imported raw silk.

Chastleton House, Oxfordshire · Black mulberry · *Morus nigra · Family: Moraceae (mulberry) · Deciduous · Origin: West Asia · Best seen in summer or autumn*

Opposite · Print from a set of six early engravings showing silkworm farming and silk weaving in 16th-century Florence: *Vermis sericus* (after Stradanus) by Philip Galle (1537–1612), wood and paper, 20.3 x 26.7cm, Lindisfarne Castle, Northumberland (NT 511839).

Right · Plate 129, 'Morus nigra', from *A Supplement to Medical Botany* (1794) by William Woodville, Anglesey Abbey, Cambridgeshire (NT 3124738).

129

Morus nigra

Published by D.ᵗ Woodville Feb.ʸ 1. 1792.

Young giant

It's difficult to think of this giant conifer as a youngster but it has a lot of growing still to do. Giant redwoods are the largest organisms that have ever lived on Earth, with some reaching over 80 metres tall and a mass of around 2,000 tonnes. It takes over 1,000 years to reach those dimensions and this one has been growing only since the 1850s.

During the 18th and 19th centuries supplying rare plants like this to wealthy clients became a lucrative business and nursery companies sprang up to meet demand. One of the most famous was that of John Veitch (1752–1839), who as well as being gardener and agent to Sir Thomas Dyke Acland of Killerton (1722–85), established a plant nursery at nearby Budlake. As trade grew, the company expanded, even employing its own 'plant hunters'. One of these, Cornish botanist William Lobb (1809–64), joined the botanical 'goldrush' of the 1850s and succeeded in collecting giant redwood in California's Sierra Nevada Mountains. This is thought to be one of them.

Killerton, Devon · Giant redwood · *Sequoiadendron giganteum* · *Family: Cupressaceae (cypress)* · *Origin: USA (California)* · *Evergreen* · *Introduced to UK: 1853*

Holm truths

Estimated to be around 400 years old, this holm oak is one of the oldest of the species in the UK, probably predating the garden. Many visitors are surprised to discover that it is an oak, especially in winter, when its appearance and evergreen habit challenge all preconceptions about what an oak tree should look like.

Large evergreen trees like this magnificent individual were highly valued by garden creators in the 17th and 18th centuries and it was quite common to incorporate existing trees into new gardens. As long as they complemented the new design, they provided immediate maturity and seasonal continuity. It does, however, make the ageing of trees difficult as they are often assumed to date from the time of the garden's establishment. Various growth formulae have been devised to estimate tree age, but growth rates vary greatly depending on environmental and soil conditions. Counting growth rings from bores or after felling is of limited use in very old trees like this due to hollowing of the trunk.

There are over 500 species of oak in the world and a large proportion are evergreen. The leaves of this species (*Quercus ilex*) are leathery and variably spiny (overleaf), explaining the second part of the botanical name, *ilex* being the generic name for holly.

The appearance of our gardens has changed through the centuries, influenced by design trends and fashions. As well as the layout of physical features and planting, the palette of plants has changed as new species have become available or increased in popularity. Trees are often the most conspicuous plants and thus the most important in providing a visual 'key' to a garden's historical origins. Maintaining trees like this holm oak, rather than introducing species that were not available when the garden was created, is therefore important in maintaining a distinctive historical spirit of place.

Westbury Court Garden, Gloucestershire · Holm oak · *Quercus ilex · Family: Fagaceae (beech) · Evergreen · Origin: southern Europe and the Mediterranean · Introduced to UK: 16th century*

Well-connected Victorian

Rhododendrons are usually thought of as sprawling shrubs but many of the world's 1,000 or so species grow to a considerable size. They were very fashionable in the 19th century, boosted by the arrival of new species from southern Asia. This one, like many others, was collected by eminent botanist and Director of Kew Gardens Joseph Hooker (1817–1911). Hooker was a friend of Charles Darwin (1809–82) and his wife Emma (1808–96), and gave several rhododendrons to them as gifts. This plant was almost certainly one of them, later given to Charles's sister Caroline Wedgwood (1800–88). In 1864 Emma Darwin wrote to Hooker: 'We have just received a blossom of *Rhododendron falconeri* which has flowered in the open air at my brother's on Leith Hill Surrey.'

Hooker named this species after palaeontologist Hugh Falconer (1808–65), a creationist opposed to Darwin's ideas of evolution. After reading Darwin's *The Origin of Species*, Falconer was won over and clearly saw how it explained his observations on fossils.

Leith Hill, Surrey · Hooker's Rhododendron ·
Rhododendron falconeri · Family: Ericaceae (heather) ·
Evergreen · Origin: Nepal, India (Sikkim) and Bhutan ·
Introduced to UK: 1850

Phoenix tree

There are many tall and impressive lime trees in Dyrham Park, but this must be the most characterful. One of its long, horizontally spreading limbs dips to the ground before shooting up again with renewed vigour. Small-leaved lime is the most common of our native limes, occurring mostly in the warmer woodlands of southern Britain, but this tree was probably planted here as an ornamental parkland specimen. The leaves (overleaf) can be identified by their heart-like (cordate) shape and delicate texture. In summer, its scented flowers are an irresistible attraction to bees, which create a soft buzz in the air and deliciously flavoured lime honey.

Between 5,000 and 7,500 years ago, during the so-called Atlantic Period, the climate of Britain was warmer than it is now. Pollen records tell us that lime was the dominant woodland tree over much of north-western Europe. As the climate cooled, its range became more restricted, partly due to its need for warm summers to ripen the seed. The trees became increasingly reliant on layering, whereby new roots are produced when limbs come into contact with the ground. This allows them to continuously regenerate, and some limes are thought to originate from ancient roots that are thousands of years old. As today's climate change brings warmer summers, lime may become a more common woodland tree again.

Dyrham Park, Gloucestershire · Small-leaved lime ·
*Tilia cordata · Family: Malvaceae (mallow) · Deciduous ·
Origin: Europe · Best seen in summer for flowers*

Fruitful retirement

Nobody is quite sure how old these apple trees are but they were probably among the first additions to Llanerchaeron's walled garden when it was created over 200 years ago. They have recently been identified through DNA analysis and include a number of old varieties with such evocative names as Kerry Pippin, Rymer and Adam's Pearmain. These ancient trees have now reached retirement, released from the servitude of annual harvest to live out a more relaxed old age. But the signs of hard labour are still visible in their gnarly bark and unnaturally shaped limbs, which now support a miniature rainforest of moss and polypody ferns.

Cordons and espaliers are ways of growing fruit trees to give maximum yield in a small area and at a convenient height for picking. These are 'lapsed' espaliers with vertical trunks and horizontal main branches that would have been trained to a post-and-wire framework. Mature espaliers have a beauty beyond their functional value, and they were often planted as ornamental features.

Llanerchaeron, Ceredigion · Fruit espaliers · *Malus domestica* · *Family: Rosaceae (rose)* · *Deciduous*

American cousin

This unmissable black walnut tree sprawls across the lawn at Antony House and seems to have opted for expansion by horizontal spread rather than height. It is an American cousin of the more frequently seen common walnut (*Juglans regia*) and is better known for its ornamental qualities than its nuts, which are difficult to shell and inferior in flavour. The pinnate leaves are easily distinguished from common walnut in having between 10 and 23 leaflets rather than 5, 7 or 9. This tree was planted in the 1790s around the time when Reginald Pole-Carew (1753–1835) of Antony House commissioned leading garden designer Humphry Repton (1752–1818) to remodel the garden in the new Picturesque style. In autumn its leaves turn a bright yellow before falling to reveal a skeleton of branches that appear to claw the winter sky.

Walnut wood has been described as a furniture-maker's dream. It is durable, stable and with a grain of infinitely varying colour and patterning. It was especially popular in the early 18th century, often used for Queen Anne and early Georgian furniture. Examples can be seen in the house at Antony, including a beautiful walnut escritoire or writing desk.

Gardeners often say that 'nothing grows under a walnut tree'. There's some truth in

this, since walnuts produce a toxic substance known as juglone that inhibits the growth of surrounding plants. Black walnut produces especially high concentrations of this natural herbicide, which is released from the roots and fallen leaves.

Antony, Cornwall · Black walnut · *Juglans nigra · Family: Juglandaceae (walnut) · Deciduous · Origin: eastern and central USA · Introduced to UK: c.1686*

Opposite · Late 17th-century staircase with balusters of black walnut from America (NT 456464) at Dyrham Park, Gloucestershire. The staircase and its expertly applied woodgraining have been revitalised as part of a recent conservation programme.

Right · Plate 1, 'Juglans nigra', from *Histoire des Arbres Forestiers de l'Amérique Septentrionale*, vol. 1 (1812) by François André-Michaux, Anglesey Abbey, Cambridgeshire (NT 3101525).

JUGLANS nigra
Black Walnut

Royal roots

This unassuming oak tree grows on a gravelled path only a stone's throw from Beningbrough Hall. It was planted here in 1898 by the then Duke of Cambridge (1819–1904), great-grandson of George III (1738–1820). It is said that the Duke was suffering from hay fever at the time and didn't want to aggravate the condition by walking across the grass. He planted the tree by the path instead, hence its unusual position. Given that it's over 120 years old, you may be surprised that it isn't bigger. The reason is that this is an unusual variegated form of common oak that grows more slowly than trees with normal leaves. If you look carefully at the trunk, you'll notice a swelling at around waist height. This is a graft line showing where the variegated portion has been grafted onto the rootstock of a normal tree.

The planting of commemorative trees is a popular way to mark a particular moment in time or a visit by a famous person. Trees are ideally suited to the purpose, combining qualities of both permanence and growth. Many National Trust properties have trees planted by famous people or to mark significant events.

Beningbrough Hall, Gallery and Gardens, North Yorkshire · Duke of Cambridge Oak · *Quercus robur 'Variegata'* · *Family: Fagaceae (beech)* · *Deciduous* · *Best seen in summer for distinctive leaves*

A world of its own

Calke Park was designated a National Nature Reserve in 2006 in recognition of its importance to nature conservation. At the time, there was a competition to name its oldest tree and this veteran oak became known as the Old Man of Calke. He's over 1,000 years old and is a relic of the ancient wood pasture that predates even the abbey itself. Many centuries of pollarding have given him a squat, tree-man appearance like a character from a fairy tale.

Ancient and veteran trees like this are nature reserves in their own right thanks to the variety of valuable habitats found within their minibeast-scale landscapes of nooks and crannies (overleaf). Dead and decaying wood are especially important for specialised invertebrates that rely on this increasingly rare habitat. There are around 350 species of beetles alone living in the veteran trees at Calke, including rarities such as the cobweb beetle (*Ctesias serra*). The care of trees like this involves protecting these habitats by leaving dead limbs unpruned or where they fall to the ground, and by preventing shading by taller trees. It's also important to look after the area around the tree to prevent compaction or use of agricultural chemicals that can damage the fungi and other soil life on which the trees rely for nutrient supply.

Calke Abbey, Derbyshire · The Old Man of Calke (Oak) · *Quercus robur · Family: Fagaceae (beech) · Deciduous*

Purple power

In spring and summer these magnificent beech trees stand out like beacons among the thousands of shades of green on display in the treescape of Waddesdon Manor. Copper or purple beech is similar in every respect to common beech except for the remarkable leaves, which open a beautiful greenish-bronze, then turn gradually to deep purple. Looking upwards from the base of the trunk reveals a colossal structure of repeatedly forking branches supporting the canopy of leaves required to power the tree's growth and reproduction.

Most trees appear green due to the dominance of the pigment chlorophyll, which is needed to harness the power of sunlight to convert water and CO_2 into sugar. We see green because that is the part of the light spectrum that green leaves do not absorb but reflect. In nature, purple-leaved individuals occasionally arise with higher-than-normal levels of other pigments called carotenoids. These red, yellow and orange pigments are present even in green leaves but are usually masked by chlorophyll. In autumn, as chlorophyll breaks down, these other pigments become visible. This explains the wonderful palette of colours displayed by this and the other deciduous trees.

As well as providing energy through sugar production, photosynthesis is the process by which a tree builds its physical structure. Carbon from the atmosphere is absorbed as CO_2 and converted into the various compounds and tissues that form the structure of the wood. On average, carbon makes up about 50 per cent of the mass of wood, which is why planting and growing trees is seen as one way to reduce the effects of climate change. 'Locking up' the stored carbon by using the timber in buildings and other long-lived structures enhances the benefits further.

Waddesdon Manor, Buckinghamshire · Copper beeches · *Fagus sylvatica 'Atropurpurea Group'* · *Family: Fagaceae (beech)* · *Deciduous* · *Best seen in May to November*

Playing with fire

Some trees fail to reach their full stature in the soils and climates of foreign lands. That is certainly not the case with Monterey pine, as proved by this colossal example in Northern Ireland. Pines are not easy to tell apart, but the dark, deeply ridged bark is a reliable identification feature of this species. Looking up into the massive crown, you will also see clusters of cones closely hugging the branches.

In the wild, Monterey pine is a rare tree with a very restricted distribution among a few cliffs on the Monterey Peninsula in California. Fires are a natural and regular occurrence, and the cones are serotinous, meaning that they remain closed until activated by intense heat to release their seed to germinate on the burnt forest floor.

Although it is rare in the wild, Monterey pine has become a major commercial forestry species in many warm temperate countries, including New Zealand, where it is the most planted tree. The wood is used for constructing timber-framed houses and general joinery.

Mount Stewart, County Down · Monterey pine · *Pinus radiata* · *Family: Pinaceae (pine)* · *Evergreen* · *Origin: USA (California)* · *Introduced to UK: 1833*

All in a row

Some trees lend themselves naturally to standing, well-behaved, in the straight lines of avenues and other formal landscape features. European lime, with its impressive height, predictable shape and 'tidy' branching habit has all the right qualities. It is a hybrid of our two native limes: small-leaved and broad-leaved. Avenue trees like these are usually propagated by cutting and grafting from a single individual, resulting in clones of uniform shape and size. This avenue was planted in 1840 and is the longest of its kind in Europe. Its 1,296 trees were arranged in double rows to add scale and dramatic effect.

Through the centuries, avenues have gone in and out of fashion depending on the prevailing artistic influences of the time. 17th- and early 18th-century ideas of formal order and control over nature gave way to a more romantic and contemplative appreciation and coexistence, leading to more naturalistic gardens. Different landscape styles often become overlaid on top of each other, and this can be seen in the various phases of tree-planting at Clumber Park: informality in the pleasure grounds contrasting with formal avenues elsewhere.

Lime wood has many practical and artistic applications. The inner layer of bark, known

as bast, has been used since Neolithic times for making rope and bindings for tools and weapons. In North America lime trees are referred to as basswood for this reason. The wood itself is perfect for turning and intricate carving with hand tools and was often used for ornamental panelling and screens in churches and stately homes. The Anglo-Dutch carver Grinling Gibbons (1648–1721) used lime wood for his famous carvings in St Paul's Cathedral and the Carved Room at Petworth House, West Sussex (opposite).

Clumber Park, Nottinghamshire · Lime Tree Avenue · *Tilia x europaea · Family: Malvaceae (mallow) · Deciduous · Origin: Europe (parent species: Tilia cordata and Tilia platyphyllos) · Best seen in summer and autumn*

Left · Plate V, 'Lime', from *The Spirit of the Woods* (1837) by Rebecca Hey, Anglesey Abbey, Cambridgeshire (NT 3101594).

Opposite · Detail of a lime-wood carving of musical instruments (c.1692) by Grinling Gibbons on the east wall of the Carved Room at Petworth House, West Sussex.

The tree that is a forest

Big conifers are a feature of the Stourhead landscape (overleaf), and this is one of the most awe-inspiring. Although not as tall as the redwoods and firs, its multiple curving trunks seem to form a small forest all of their own. Western red cedar is a kind of cypress with sprays of scale-like leaves rather than the needles of a true cedar. There are several species of cypress and they can be tricky to tell apart. Smell can be a useful clue and the crushed foliage of this species has a fruity scent that for many evokes childhood memories of traditional 'pineapple chunk' sweets.

Western red cedar is an amazingly useful tree. The Native American people of coastal Oregon and Alaska sometimes refer to themselves as 'the people of the red cedar' because of the fundamental role the tree and its products has played in their lives and culture. The timber has been used for construction as well as for cooking utensils, boxes, musical instruments, canoes and totem poles. The leaves and bark also have a wide variety of medicinal applications.

The wood contains chemicals called thujaplicins, which act as natural fungicides and resist rotting. This makes it an ideal material for window frames, cladding and glasshouse structures.

Stourhead, Wiltshire · Western red cedar · *Thuja plicata* · *Family: Cupressaceae (cypress)* · *Evergreen* · *Origin: western North America* · *Introduced to UK: 1853*

Signpost to the past

The landscape of Stowe has changed dramatically over the last three centuries as successive owners have reshaped it to their own tastes and ambitions. Historical records can help us to understand these changes but there are also subtle clues left behind in the landscape. One remnant of earlier times is this ancient oak tree, named the Farey Oak after a former tenant of the land on which it resides. It is thought to be an old way-marker that once stood alongside the ancient road that ran between Buckingham and Towcester, connecting the small village of Lamport. A roadside commissioner's report from the late 18th century mentions a 'great big oak tree' that stood on the side of a road. The road has gone, along with the village itself, which was abandoned in around 1850 following gradual enclosure of the common land and expansion of the deer park by the Temples, owners of Stowe Park.

Before reliable maps and signs were available, trees were often used as way-markers or indicators of ownership or parish boundaries. Their size and longevity make them ideal for the purpose, and generations of landowners and managers would retain them in the landscape, often as pollards. This tree is thought to be almost 700 years old.

Stowe, Buckinghamshire · The Farey Oak · *Quercus robur · Family: Fagaceae (beech) · Deciduous*

The Fraternal Four

It takes a bit of effort to visit these four ancient yew trees, which are tucked away high in the Lake District's Seathwaite Valley. When you get there, however, it's like entering a fairy-tale world of ancient tree-people shaped by the valley's rocky soil and harsh climate. William Wordsworth (1770–1850) referred to the trees as 'The Fraternal Four', describing the scene in his poem 'Yew Trees' (1803):

Joined in one solemn and capacious grove
Huge trunks! – and each particular trunk a growth
Of intertwisted fibres serpentine
Up-coiling and inveterately convolved.

One of the four has lain on its side since 1883, when it was blown over and uprooted in a great storm. Its trunk has been gradually decaying ever since but can still be seen.

Yew is the longest-lived of all our native trees. Estimating the age of hollow ancient trees like these is a challenge, especially as growth rates vary widely, depending on soil conditions and exposure. A section of intact wood from the fallen tree has been examined to measure its growth rate and thereby its age. It is estimated to have been around 1,000 years old when it was uprooted.

In Celtic mythology yew trees were closely associated with death and resurrection. The foliage and seeds are toxic, while its longevity and ability to regenerate itself from fallen limbs help to explain this fascination and reverence.

Borrowdale, Cumbria · Ancient yews · *Taxus baccata* · *Taxaceae (yew)* · *Evergreen* · *Origin: Europe, West Asia, North Africa*

Right · A view of the Borrowdale Yews and Seathwaite Valley captured around the turn of the 20th century by the Ambleside photographer Herbert Bell (1856–1946). Bell and his brothers walked and climbed the fells with camping equipment and heavy cameras, tripods and glass plates, using their canvas tent as a mobile darkroom.

Innovative newcomer

It is often assumed that conifers are evergreen but some species buck the trend by evolving a deciduous habit. The dawn redwood is one of them and the tawny pink of its turning autumn foliage is one of its most beautiful features. It was introduced to Britain in 1947, quickly becoming popular in parks and gardens for its fast growth, attractive foliage and fluted rusty-brown bark. The species only became known to science in 1941, when Chinese forestry professor Toh Kan (Duo Gan, 1903–61) observed an unfamiliar tree while surveying in a remote area of central China. Even now, new species are being discovered and introduced to cultivation.

The evolutionary 'decision' between deciduous or evergreen habits is driven by a combination of climatic and environmental factors. In constant environments such as warm temperate ones, most trees opt for an evergreen strategy, investing resources in durable, long-lasting leaves. In more seasonally extreme climates, it is more economic to grow 'disposable' leaves that are replaced each year.

Sheffield Park and Garden, East Sussex · Dawn redwood · *Metasequoia glyptostroboides* · *Cupressaceae (cypress)* · *Deciduous* · *Origin: central China* · *Introduced to UK: 1947*

Floral paradise

The garden at Nymans has an international reputation for its rare and exotic trees and shrubs. Magnolias provide a wonderful display from late winter through spring, and one of the most conspicuous is this magnificent tree. Its flowers arrive in April or early May, before the leaves, and resemble large, pink-flushed water lilies (overleaf). It was planted in the 1920s and first flowered in 1932, when Nymans was enjoying a period of renaissance and expansion under the ownership of Leonard and Maud Messel (1872–1953 and 1875–1960 respectively). The couple shared a great love of magnolias, and several popular hybrids and cultivars are closely associated with them and Nymans, including *Magnolia x loebneri* 'Leonard Messel', a number of which can be seen in the garden.

Although named after the eminent American botanist Charles Sprague Sargent (1841–1927), this species was first introduced to Britain by the prolific plant collector Ernest Henry Wilson (1876–1930). Wilson is best known for his botanical expeditions to China in the early years of the 20th century, which were sponsored by commercial nurseries and private collectors. He is credited with introducing over 1,000 plant species to Britain, including many of our most familiar garden plants. Leonard Messel sponsored Wilson's collecting trips and received many plants in return.

Nymans, West Sussex · Sargent's Magnolia · *Magnolia sargentiana var. robusta* · *Family: Magnoliaceae (magnolia)* · *Deciduous* · *Origin: China (western Sichuan)* · *Introduced to UK: 1908* · *Best seen in spring for flowers*

Shapely veteran

This 200-year-old tree grows on the expanse of lawn behind Gunby Hall in Lincolnshire and is often said to be one of the finest cedars of Lebanon in the British Isles. It was planted between 1810 and 1815 by Peregrine Langton-Massingberd (1780–1858), then owner of Gunby Hall. It has the characteristic shape of cedar trees, with a massive trunk, arching limbs and layered parasols of foliage. Many cedars of this age bear the wounds of high winds and heavy snowfalls, but this tree has shown remarkable resilience and maintains its magnificent form and shape despite its longevity.

The woody framework of a tree like this needs to be immensely strong to support the colossal weight of its branches and foliage.

In windy conditions or when snow settles on the flat branches the forces are multiplied. Evolution has given trees like this a structure that engineers describe as 'shape-optimised': the tree lays down additional wood, resulting in tapering and flaring of the trunk and branches in the areas of greatest stress. Nature provides many examples of shape-optimised structures, including deer antlers and the claws of big cats.

Gunby Estate, Hall and Gardens, Lincolnshire · Cedar of Lebanon · *Cedrus libani · Family: Pinaceae (pine) · Evergreen · Origin: South-west Asia · Introduced to UK: c.1645*

Glossary of terms

Ancient tree · A tree that has reached a great age compared to others of its kind. The designation therefore varies from one species to another depending on its typical longevity. Short-lived trees, such as birch, are considered ancient at around 150 years old, whereas an ancient oak tree will be over 400.

Arboretum · An area of land on which many different trees or shrubs are grown for study or display. Arboretums became popular during the 18th and 19th centuries as landscape features on large private estates.

Arboriculture · The cultivation of trees and shrubs.

Broadleaved tree (angiosperm) · A tree that typically has broad fleshy leaves and flowers.

Champion tree · A tree recognised and recorded by the Tree Register of the British Isles as the largest (by height or girth) of its kind. Trees can be county or national champions.

Conifer (gymnosperm) · A tree that typically has needle- or scale-like leaves and cones.

Cultivar · A plant (including trees) that has been cloned (selected and propagated by vegetative methods) to retain desirable characteristics. In addition to their species name, cultivars are given a name that is rendered in single quotation marks, e.g. *Malus domestica* 'Flower of Kent'.

Deciduous tree · A tree that sheds its leaves annually and has a leafless season.

Dendrology · The science and study of trees and shrubs.

Evergreen tree · A tree that has leaves all year round. The leaves are kept for more than one year, with only the oldest shed each year.

Genus (plural genera) · A category used in biological classification that is above species and below family: beech (*Fagus*), oak (*Quercus*) and maple (*Acer*) are genera.

Below · Pollarded willows, River Wey and Godalming Navigations and Dapdune Wharf, Surrey.

Above · Common leaf shapes, from left to right: ovate (e.g. beech), cordate (lime), pinnate (ash), palmate (maple), digitate (horse chestnut) and lobate (oak).

Grafting · A technique for propagating plants through vegetative (non-sexual) means. A cutting (scion) from the tree to be propagated is grafted onto the roots and stem (rootstock) of a closely related but more easily available or vigorous tree to produce identical clones of the original.

Leaf · The main organ of photosynthesis and transpiration in higher plants. The shape and arrangement of leaves on a stem (above) is the most common means of identifying a tree.

Photosynthesis · The process by which plants synthesise sugar from CO_2 and water using the power of sunlight.

Pollard · A tree that has been managed by regular pruning at around head height to yield a regular harvest of branches and foliage (opposite). Pollarding is a traditional system of managing trees within parks and landscapes shared by trees and domestic animals, and differs from coppicing in the height of cutting to prevent the grazing of young shoots.

Shrub · A woody plant that is smaller than a tree and has several main stems arising at or near the ground.

Species · The most basic category used to classify plants and animals; e.g. field maple (*Acer campestre*) is a species in the maple genus. The species name is shown after the genus.

Tree · A large woody perennial plant, typically with one main stem or trunk. You can climb a tree but not a shrub.

Veteran tree · A tree that shows the characteristics of ageing, including cavities, hollowing and deadwood. These are also typical of ancient trees but veteran status is not defined by age.

Wood · The hard fibrous material that forms the trunk or branches of a tree or shrub.

Gazetteer of National Trust Places

The following gazetteer provides a brief introduction to the National Trust places featured in this book and to others where visitors will find significant individual trees or tree and plant collections of special interest. For full details of every National Trust property, including further information about gardens, collections, opening times, events and facilities, please visit the National Trust website (www.nationaltrust.org.uk).

Aira Force, Cumbria
This 18th-century Picturesque-style pleasure ground with panoramic views over Ullswater was developed by Charles Howard, 11th Duke of Norfolk, for visitors to the family's hunting lodge at Lyulph's Tower. It was a place for exploration, trepidation and excitement, a journey from the beautiful to the sublime. Quiet glades give way to dramatic waterfalls in this landscape of contrasts. The arboretum includes a fine collection of specimen conifers (firs, pines, spruces and cedars) from all over the world.

Antony, Cornwall
Antony House has been the family seat of the Carew family since the 16th century, when they gained power and influence at the court of Henry VIII. The 3rd Baronet commissioned Humphry Repton to design the formal gardens and grounds, which are situated to the west and north-west of the house and comprise formal terraces and lawns adjacent to the house, together with pleasure grounds and woodland gardens. Trees of note include cedar of Lebanon, paperbark maple and an American black walnut planted in the 1790s.

Belton House, Lincolnshire
The first formal gardens at Belton were destroyed by a devastating flood. The new fashion for 'natural' landscapes left behind a small canal to the north-east of the house and an extensive parkland. This includes a sweeping double avenue of lime and chestnut trees and an arboretum. Later generations of the Brownlow family returned to the original formal idea with the sunken Italian Garden, designed by Jeffry Wyatville in the early 19th century, and the Dutch Garden, commissioned by the 3rd Earl Brownlow in 1880 to harmonise with the north front of the house.

Beningbrough Hall, Gallery and Gardens, North Yorkshire
Fragments of Beningbrough's 18th-century fabric survive in the mature yew trees, serpentine path and garden walls. Later features include an arch of pear trees planted in the 1890s and a

glasshouse containing a 'Foster's Seedling' grapevine, bred by head gardener Thomas Foster in 1835. The 8-acre formal garden includes beds and borders, the wide gravel path of the South Terrace with views over the parkland, and an American Garden featuring magnolia, rhododendron and liriodendron.

Biddulph Grange Garden, Staffordshire

James Bateman bought the estate in 1840 and subsequently built up the gardens, creating a masterpiece of Victorian design inspired by his millenarian beliefs and his desire to create microclimates to display and cultivate fascinating plants, including monkey puzzle trees. Bateman commissioned plant-collecting expeditions all over the world. The gardens, which include tunnels, a yew pyramid, a Cheshire cottage and a Chinese bridge and garden, are a rare survivor of High Victorian design and home to one of the Trust's major plant collections.

Bodnant Garden, Conwy

Bodnant has an internationally renowned plant collection. A Grade I registered landscape extending to 80 acres, much of the design was influenced by Edward Milner, Thomas Mawson and William Robinson. The garden became a centre of botanical enterprise, sponsoring plant-hunting expeditions and setting up a plant-breeding programme. It includes grand formal terraces, the ravine-like Dell Garden and highlights such as the 55m-long Laburnum Arch.

Above · A topiary-lined path in the Italian Garden at Belton House, Lincolnshire.

Trees of note include Japanese umbrella pine and unusual species of maple and rowan.

Borrowdale, Cumbria

Borrowdale has the largest area of native broadleaf woodland of any of the Lake District valleys. In autumn the valley fills with waves of colour as the birches, wild cherry, ash and finally the oaks put on their display. These woodlands are the last surviving fragments of an enormous ancient forest that once stretched down the west coast of Britain and Ireland. They receive 3.5m of rainfall per year, qualifying as temperate rainforest as a result. The woods in this valley are among the most important habitats in Europe for mosses, liverworts (bryophytes) and lichens.

Calke Abbey, Derbyshire

Calke came into the ownership of the Harpur family in 1622. It stayed in the family until the National Trust began caring for it in 1985. The Trust decided not to restore the rooms but to preserve them as found. This philosophy is also reflected in areas of the garden, where peeling paintwork in the Orangery and old potting sheds contrast with the flower and kitchen gardens. Once an extensive pleasure ground, the gardens feature tunnels designed to hide the gardeners from view. Ancient oak, sweet and horse chestnut trees can be found in the parkland.

Chastleton House, Oxfordshire

Chastleton is a Grade II* registered Jacobean country house garden that includes a pleasure garden, kitchen garden, orchard and extensive parkland. The 19th-century topiary of the Best Garden once featured shapes including a cake-stand and a ship in full sail. The wider historic parkland is the setting for the Boscobel Oak, grown by John and Dorothy Whitmore-Jones in 1852 from an acorn from the Royal Oak of Boscobel. To the north-east of the house is a characterful black mulberry, which

Above · A pair of conjoined ancient yew trees at Crom, County Fermanagh.

continues to thrive despite being blown over by a storm in 2000.

Clumber Park, Nottinghamshire

This extensive ancient estate, which once belonged to the Dukes of Newcastle, covers more than 3,800 acres. Although the estate is largely intact, the mansion and formal gardens were dismantled in the late 1930s. The pleasure ground consists of the remains of the formal features, picturesque walks, beautiful specimen trees and garden temples on the north bank of an artificial lake. The parkland includes a number of avenues, including almost 2 miles of lime trees planted in the 19th century, as well as peaceful oak woodlands.

Cragside, Northumberland

Cragside is a testament to the vision and energy of its creators, Lord and Lady Armstrong. Lord Armstrong created five lakes across the estate and harnessed their power to generate hydroelectricity to light the mansion. The Armstrongs planted 7 million trees and shrubs, including hundreds of hardy hybrid rhodo-dendrons and a 2.4-acre pinetum containing specimen conifers. A terraced formal garden was created to take advantage of the sunny, open views to the south. This contained ranges of ornamental glasshouses, carpet beds and a kitchen garden.

Crom, County Fermanagh

A 2,000-acre estate made up of tranquil islands and ancient woodlands in one of Ireland's most important conservation areas. The 17th-century castle was destroyed by a fire in 1764 but the ruins survive, forming a romantic monument in the landscape. Crom is home to a pair of conjoined yew trees with a combined circumference of 115m and a diameter of 35m.

Croome, Worcestershire

An extensive landscape parkland designed around the mid-18th-century Neo-Palladian mansion Croome Court. Both the mansion and the park were designed by Lancelot 'Capability' Brown for the 6th Earl of Coventry, and Croome was Brown's first major commission. The parkland features numerous 'eye-catchers', including the Church of St Mary Magdalene and a variety of water courses, lakes and bridges. The extensive plant collection, including ginkgo trees and deciduous swamp cypress, was once described as rivalling Kew's.

Dinefwr, Carmarthenshire

This Grade I registered park is steeped in myth and history. Extending to 800 acres, the gardens of Dinefwr are home to the ruins of Dinefwr Castle and were laid out in the 18th century to the recommendations of 'Capability' Brown. Home to a herd of fallow deer and rare breed White Park cattle, it is the only parkland nature reserve in Wales, with over 300 oak trees of at least 400 years old, ancient pasture and rare fungi.

Dunham Massey, Cheshire

This 300-acre estate was once home to two influential families, the Booths and the Greys. The ancient deer park was enclosed in 1751 but today visitors can wander among the wildlife through lime avenues and ancient oak trees. The high water-table in the garden favours moisture-loving shrubs, perennials and ferns, giving the planting a lush feel, while the acidic soil conditions allow azaleas to flourish. The Winter Garden, designed by plantsman Roy Lancaster, contains fragrant shrubs and over 200,000 bulbs, providing a great spectacle in late winter and early spring.

Dyffryn Gardens, Vale of Glamorgan

In the early 20th century the industrialist Cory family built a large house at Dyffryn with a grand Edwardian garden designed by Thomas Mawson. The landscape to the north of the house is largely of this older character. Later areas of development to the south and west include an arboretum, the informal West Garden and formal south lawns, terraces and garden 'rooms'. There are two walled gardens and a glasshouse complex, containing orchid and cacti collections. The plant collection is of significant interest and includes several original introductions from China, such as the paperbark maple tree.

Dyrham Park, Gloucestershire

Dyrham Park has been shaped by hundreds of years of enclosure and occupation. The Tudor mansion was transformed by William Blathwayt, who commissioned the notable designers of the period, including George London, to develop one of the grandest Dutch-style gardens of the late 17th century. Today, various garden phases can be seen, including remnants of the extensive formal tree avenues. The parkland's majestic mature trees include horse chestnut, sweet chestnut, oak, ash and lime. Since its acquisition, the National Trust has been

steadily conserving and reopening more of Dyrham Park, informed by new research and archaeological investigations.

Emmetts Garden, Kent

The garden is the creation of Frederic Lubbock, a banker who bought the property in 1893, but the design was heavily influenced by his friend William Robinson from nearby Gravetye Manor. The garden follows a pattern of lawns, glades and meandering paths, with the only formal elements being the Rose Garden and Rock

Below · Fountains Abbey and Studley Royal water garden, North Yorkshire.

Garden. The sloping garden is home to a collection of trees and shrubs, such as Japanese maples and a Chilean lantern tree, which have been planted with ample space to flourish and so that visitors can admire them from all angles.

Erddig, Wrexham

The early 18th-century layout of the Dutch-style garden is set around an ornamental canal with formal gardens punctuated by Irish yew topiary. The garden's restoration was based on a 1739 plan and on 19th- and 20th-century illustrations. Winding woodland walks lead visitors past ancient oaks to the unusual 'cup and saucer' water feature, where the Black Brook flows into a circular pond to cascade through a hole in its centre.

Florence Court, County Fermanagh

The house sits in a rugged wilderness at the base of the mountains of Cuilcagh. It was built in the mid-18th century for John Cole, governor of Enniskillen, and the parkland was landscaped for his son in 1778. The demesne is home to the original Irish yew, grown from a pair in the local area in around 1770, as well as several fine specimens of weeping beech. The gardens consist of a formal pleasure ground facing the mountains and a large rose garden, an orchard of traditional and Irish varieties, and a walled garden to the south of the site. The Victorian sawmill and hydraulic ram have recently been restored.

Fountains Abbey and Studley Royal Water Garden, North Yorkshire

The UNESCO World Heritage Site of 'Studley Royal Park including the ruins of Fountains Abbey' is the extraordinary creation of John Aislabie and his son William. Its development began in 1718, when John started work to transform the rugged valley of the River Skell. From 1768 the project continued under William, who purchased the ruins of the Abbey in 1762. Elements of the 18th-century landscape are remarkably intact, including the bosquet hedges, mirror lakes and moon-shaped ponds of the Studley Royal water garden, and the deer park with its lime avenues and ancient sweet chestnut trees.

Gibside, Tyne and Wear

Gibside is a Grade I registered garden and one of the most significant surviving 18th-century designed landscapes in the UK. The estate occupies 600 acres on an elevated position above the River Derwent. It includes a 4-acre walled garden, an orangery, parklands and a series of veteran and champion trees. An avenue of oaks, sycamores and limes links the Chapel and the Column to Liberty. Commissioned by coal baron George Bowes in the 1730s, the estate offers a glimpse of the compelling story of heiress Mary Eleanor Bowes, who commissioned international plant expeditions to search for new and rare species.

Glendurgan Garden, Cornwall

A garden created in three valleys, Glendurgan was designed by the wealthy Fox family. Thanks to its mild climate, plants from the southern hemisphere bloom alongside native species. The layout of principal walks was established by Alfred Fox and rare plants were acquired through the family's shipping interests. The property passed to the fifth son, George, who was a keen botanist. Under his ownership, the plant collection was maintained and expanded, with a particular emphasis on conifers and tender rhododendrons. Cuthbert Fox succeeded George and continued to develop the garden, which the family presented to the National Trust in 1962. Magnolias and tree ferns enhance its exotic atmosphere.

Greenway, Devon

The Greenway estate has had several owners, notably the author Agatha Christie and her husband Max Mallowan. Successive owners brought new additions to the walled gardens and parkland, including specimens from nurseries across the country. Exotic species were introduced by Mary Bolitho from plant collector George Forrest's early 20th-century expeditions to Yunnan. Alongside the hardy perennials, rhododendrons, magnolias and impressive Victorian fernery, visitors can see the 19th-century boathouse that featured in Christie's novel *Dead Man's Folly*.

Gunby Estate, Hall and Gardens, Lincolnshire

Gunby Hall was the home of the Massingberd family for more than 250 years. In 1802 Elizabeth Mary Anne Massingberd married Peregrine Langton, who recorded all the tree-planting on the estate in *The Gunby Tree Book*. Langton's passion was creating new plantations and he was greatly assisted in this by the nurseryman and landscape designer William Pontey. Pontey advised Langton to plant belts of trees with breaks in them to focus views on distant landmarks, giving the impression of a more generously wooded landscape. Apple, pear, plum and fig trees can be found in the kitchen garden. An impressive 200-year-old cedar of Lebanon stands behind the Hall.

Hadrian's Wall and Housesteads Fort, Northumberland

The UNESCO World Heritage Site of Hadrian's Wall runs 73 miles across the country from Wallsend in the east to Bowness-on-Solway in the west. Work started on the wall during the reign of the Emperor Hadrian in AD 122 and the Romans continued to be a presence along this frontier for the next 300 years. The Housesteads estate encompasses a 6-mile section of Hadrian's Wall where it runs along the crest of a rocky outcrop known as the Whin Sill. The line of this ridge is interrupted in places by distinctive notches caused by erosion from glacial meltwater. One of the National Trust's

Above · The hornbeam arch running alongside the cherry garden at Ham House, Surrey, in winter.

most famous trees stands at Sycamore Gap near Crag Lough, Northumberland.

Ham House and Garden, Surrey

17th-century character and contemporary gardening approaches combine in this recreated garden on the banks of the River Thames. A 2-acre kitchen garden with orchard, a formal parterre displaying over 1,200 lavenders among topiary box and a wilderness woodland with hornbeam and field maple surround the 17th-century grass lawns. Known as 'plats', the lawns are planted with over half a million successively flowering spring bulbs, and include significant areas of wildflower meadow.

Hatfield Forest National Nature Reserve, Essex

A rare surviving example of a medieval royal hunting forest, with over 1,000 acres of coppices and wood pasture. The Georgian period saw the creation of a designed landscape at Hatfield, including interventions by Lancelot 'Capability' Brown. During the Victorian era it was drained and protected from conversion to agricultural use, and exotic specimen trees, such as horse chestnuts, planes and firs, were planted alongside the ancient oaks and hornbeams. Hatfield Forest was sold to a timber merchant in the early 1920s but was saved from large-scale felling by the pioneering conservationist Edward North Buxton. After Buxton's death the forest was bequeathed to the National Trust, which opened it to the public in 1924.

Hidcote, Gloucestershire

A significant Arts and Crafts garden set around a 17th-century farmhouse. In 1907 Lawrence Johnston created one of the country's most notable Arts and Crafts gardens on the relatively untouched site, consisting of a series of outdoor 'rooms', long hedged walks and colour-themed borders. By the early 1920s the garden design was largely complete. Johnston's interests then moved on to international plant-hunting. At his suggestion, the National Trust assumed custodianship in 1948. It was the first garden of national importance to be taken on under the Gardens Fund, established by the National Trust and the Royal Horticultural Society to save significant gardens. Hidcote's Japanese hill cherry is a particular spring highlight.

High Close Estate, Cumbria

Originally planted in 1866 by Edward Wheatley-Balme, a Yorkshire merchant and philanthropist, High Close was designed in the fashion of the day using many of the recently discovered 'exotic' conifers and evergreen shrubs arriving from America. The exposed location of the garden has resulted in some losses but there are still many fine specimens, including Douglas firs, Sitka spruce and redwoods. The setting of this mid-Victorian Lake District villa is unusual, eschewing the archetypal lakeside aspect in favour of a valley in the High Fells that commands a panorama stretching from the Langdale valley to Windermere.

Hinton Ampner, Hampshire

Hinton Ampner was the design masterpiece of Ralph Dutton, the 8th and last Lord Sherborne. The gardens united a formal layout of immaculate hedges and topiary with varied and informal plantings in mainly pastel shades. It is a garden of considerable interest to the plant

Above • A view across Ilam Park, Derbyshire.

and tree enthusiast, with many notable species, scented plants, yew topiary, ancient oaks, sycamore, ash, black walnut, and sweet and horse chestnut. The fine lawns and terraces are complemented by magnificent vistas over the park and rolling Hampshire countryside.

Hughenden, Buckinghamshire

The estate was acquired by Benjamin Disraeli in 1848. The house is located in sweeping parkland and set off by a terrace in the Italianate style. The forecourt is High Victorian with cedars, firs and spruce set against the Gothic façade, leading round to the terrace and formal bedding parterre. Here is a carefully framed view of the parkland towards High Wycombe, known as 'the landscape window'. The walled kitchen garden, dating from 1750, has been restored and is planted with 57 local Buckinghamshire apple varieties as well as wall-trained vines, figs, Morello cherry, pears and peaches.

Ickworth, Suffolk

Designed to reflect the late 18th-century Italianate house commissioned by the eccentric 4th Earl of Bristol, Frederick Augustus Hervey, the grounds are heavily wooded with yew, evergreen oak and box. Paths provide views of the impressive central rotunda from various vantage points. There are many mature trees on the lawn in front of the rotunda, including Mediterranean pines, oaks and cedars. The park surrounding the house contains fine examples of ancient specimen trees, including oak, beech and hornbeam.

Ilam Park, Derbyshire

Lying within the Peak District National Park near Ashbourne, Ilam Park is an 18th-century landscape garden and parkland in the valley of the River Manifold. The unusual zigzag path, recently planted with 13,000 spring bulbs, predates the landscaping carried out in the 1770s and is one of the earliest features of the site. Later features include the Italian Garden with its fabulous views to the peaks beyond.

The well-maintained park includes coniferous planting and the surrounding woodlands offer an ever-changing treescape that reflects the seasons.

Kedleston Hall, Derbyshire

Completed under the watchful eye of the famous architect Robert Adam, Kedleston Hall was built for Sir Nathaniel Curzon in 1765. Today, the restored Georgian pleasure ground circuit walk follows a 3-mile winding path that connected the hall, gardens and parklands and boasted a number of features, including a Turkish tent, viewing mound, shrubbery theatre and hermitage (recently restored). An extensive ten-year planting programme seeks to recreate the atmosphere for which such circuit walks were known, leading the walker from light, open groves of scented plants to dark, enclosed tunnels through yew and box, and on to enjoy views of the wider landscape. The parkland has many ancient and veteran trees, including oaks that predate the house.

Killerton, Devon

The house and grounds were originally developed by Edward Drewe in the 16th century. In the early 17th century the house was sold to John Acland, whose son, Sir Hugh Acland, went on to develop the house and wider landscape. Sir Thomas Acland employed John Veitch in 1770 to lay out the landscape park to create the setting for the new house. Under the direction of Veitch's son James, the pleasure grounds and part of the park were planted with trees and shrubs newly introduced to cultivation by Veitch's expanding nursery. Plant collecting at Killerton continued into the 20th century funded by Sir Francis Acland, who sponsored expeditions by Frank Kingdon-Ward. The gardens and grounds contain Persian ironwood, zelkova and a grove of tulip trees.

Kingston Lacy, Dorset

Kingston Lacy was part of a medieval royal hunting estate. The park and house were developed by successive generations of the Bankes family and the garden incorporates ancient Egyptian antiquities, including a 9m-high obelisk, collected by the explorer William John Bankes. The sunken gardens include beds laid out to a design by William Goldring. Further south, Lady Walk includes an extensive Japanese garden filled with maple trees. South of the pleasure gardens is a kitchen garden that was constructed in the early 20th century for Henrietta Bankes.

Knightshayes, Devon

The original Victorian garden was designed by the celebrated landscaper Edward Kemp but the present, more extensive gardens owe much to the late Sir John and Lady Heathcoat Amory, who gave Knightshayes to the National Trust in 1972. The Amorys designed, planted and maintained growing collections of magnolia, rhododendron, unusual trees and shrubs, bulbs and herbaceous plants within their 'Garden in the Wood'. This is laid out beyond the formal lawns surrounded by battlemented yews, a topiary chase scene and a circular lily pool.

Lanhydrock, Cornwall

This Victorian garden is significant for its site, design and plant collection. It has magnificent panoramic views outward across the Fowey Valley and also inward towards the park, and it remains distinct in several components: the geographic formal parterres, sentinel Irish yews, Grade II listed bronze bagatelle urns, a pleasure ground to the west and a 'wild' or woodland garden in the Great Wood. While the design of the garden and its range of forest trees and hardy hybrid rhododendrons and camellias remain highly Victorian, its planting has continued to evolve.

Leith Hill, Surrey

Leith Hill is an attractive example of a small rural estate of rolling farmland, managed on traditional lines. Its woodland of varied character includes rhododendrons, fine oak and beech trees with glades carpeted by bluebells in spring. Young plantations of conifers nurse future crops of hardwood. Leith Hill was saved in 1923 thanks to a campaign led by local residents and the Footpaths, Commons and Open Spaces Society, the organisation in which the National Trust's founders first worked together.

Llanerchaeron, Ceredigion

An elegant Georgian villa designed by John Nash with walled gardens, farmyard and lake, set in the nature-rich Aeron Valley. The walled gardens have been producing fruit and vegetables for over 200 years and include productive kitchen gardens, ancient fruit trees, herbaceous borders and a herb garden. Technological innovations have included the use of hypocausts to aid fruit production. Ancient apple trees have been joined by new plantings and there are now

Below · A view across the lake at Mount Stewart, County Down, in autumn.

51 varieties of apple. Together with the small Georgian pleasure grounds and the farm, Llanerchaeron continues to be presented as a working, living, provincial gentleman's estate.

Mottisfont, Hampshire

Mottisfont was originally an Augustinian priory, founded in 1201 beside the River Test. It became a home under the ownership of Lord Sandys in 1536. Mottisfont changed as rapidly in style as it did in ownership before it was given to the Trust in 1957. The walled gardens are home to the National Collection of over 500 pre-1900 old-fashioned roses. The nucleus of the collection belonged to Graham Stuart Thomas, the Trust's first gardens adviser. He designed the rose garden here in the early 1970s to house his collection and it became the focus of the main garden. The property is also home to a large collection of London plane trees, distributed across the gardens and estate.

Mount Stewart, County Down

Beginning in 1921, the garden was developed and transformed by the Marchioness of Londonderry over a period of 40 years. Transferred to the National Trust in 1955, it consists of several themed 'rooms' alongside larger landscape features, including a lake and woodland walks. The garden has a strong history of design and plant collecting, and exotic species such as eucalyptus, tree ferns and bananas thrive here despite the northern location. The garden's design incorporates elements of Irish folklore, family history and mythology, and it includes an enclosed topiary garden, coloured with seasonal bedding. The garden also includes fine examples of Monterey pine, giant sequoia and holm oak.

Nymans, West Sussex

Ludwig Messel began the creation of Nymans in 1885 with his head gardener, James Comber, and it was carried on by Ludwig's son Leonard. Over a period of 75 years, the family assembled a collection of remarkable trees, shrubs and plants from all over the world, while retaining a garden of intimate charm. Part of the house was destroyed by fire in 1947 but its shell houses a new garden based on the exotics so loved by the Messel family. Although the pinetum was badly hit by the Great Storm of 1987, a new collection of over 150 varieties of conifer was planted, many propagated from the fallen trees. The garden is also home to a collection of Sussex heathers, collected and bred locally.

Osterley Park and House, Middlesex

The flowing landscape park has been cut off from its northern portion by the M4 and the remaining section is a parkland formed of flowing lakes and large meadows. The pleasure grounds blend into a pinetum. The house was refined by Robert Adam as a 'party house' for the owners, and additions to the garden reflect this, with a handsome garden house containing 45 citrus trees listed in the 1785 inventory.

Above · Powis Castle, with its clipped yews and terraces, viewed from the 'wilderness'.

Flower displays are seen today inside the large Tudor walled garden: a long cutting garden and heirloom vegetables are features here. The American Border is a popular garden element from the 18th century for displaying trees and shrubs from the New World.

Overbeck's, Devon

On a site acquired by Albert Stumbles in the late 19th century, Overbeck's was one of the first houses to be built on the steeply sloping coastline south-west of Salcombe. It was subsequently sold to Edric Hopkins, who constructed a series of terraces on the east-facing slope below the house. Hopkins purchased additional land to the south, which was laid out as a terraced tennis lawn, rocky dell and orchard. The estate was later sold to the inventor Otto Overbeck, during whose ownership new areas were converted to horticulture, and the garden, which was regularly opened to the public, became famous for its collection of subtropical plants, including palms and bananas.

Petworth, West Sussex

Petworth House features a 'Capability' Brown landscaped deer park with two lakes, tree-crowned hills and peripheral plantations, all immortalised in the paintings of J.M.W. Turner. The woodland garden, with its Doric temple and Ionic rotunda, enclosed by a ha-ha, was inspired by Brown, who also enriched the planting with exotic species of trees and shrubs, including Japanese maples, arbutus, tulip trees and chestnuts. The diversity of habitat supports a wide range of plants and the tradition of adventurous planting continues today.

Plas Newydd House and Garden, Anglesey

Much of the character of Plas Newydd, a Grade I registered landscape, remains unchanged since the late 18th century. Humphry Repton was employed to design the landscape, creating glimpsed views of the house, stable block and imposing backdrop of Snowdonia beyond. Several of Repton's original plantings of beech, sycamore and oak survive. The gardens remained little altered until the early 20th century, when the 6th Marquess created the Italianate terraces to the north of the house, together with extensive shrubberies to the south. The 7th Marquess continued developments, planting an extensive rhododendron garden and an arboretum of Australasian trees.

Polesden Lacey, Surrey

The Polesden Lacey estate was left to the National Trust in 1942 by Mrs Ronnie Greville, a well-known society hostess. The gardens, Mrs Greville's creation, are Edwardian in style, with a walled rose garden and separate lavender, iris and peony gardens. They are set within 30 acres of lawns, which include a pinetum, and there are splendid specimens of beech, oak and sycamore, typical of the chalk downland landscape.

Powis Castle and Garden, Powys

Powis Castle looks out from its rocky outcrop over the Welsh marches near the town of Welshpool. Much of the garden structure, with its walls, alcoves and statues, dates from the early 18th century, when it was set out in the then-fashionable formal style with ponds and water cascades. These water features are now lost but the grand terraces remain, having narrowly avoided being blown up on the recommendation of William Emes, who laid out the park in the later 18th-century landscape style. The garden is famous for its huge, billowy yew 'tumps', exemplar herbaceous borders and annual displays of tender exotics.

Prior Park Landscape Garden, Somerset

With breathtaking views over Bath, the current landscape dates mostly from the 18th century and was created by Ralph Allen. He began work in 1734, planting a 'wilderness' and constructing terraces and lakes. The Gothick Temple was built in 1745 and the elegant Palladian Bridge was constructed between the top and middle lakes in 1755. In 1993 the National Trust acquired 26 acres of the landscape garden, then sadly neglected, and began a lengthy programme of restoration. The woodlands are home to some fascinating specimens, including 18th-century yews.

Rainham Hall, London

Rainham Hall is a community-led garden, with a small communal growing space, nature playground, outdoor classroom and an orchard of apple, plum, mulberry and pear trees. The house, which used to be a nursery school, has a long history of community-led gardening. Rainham provides an oasis of urban green space for visitors to explore and enjoy free of charge all year round.

Rowallane Garden, County Down

Rowallane is a beautiful woodland garden and arboretum created in the late 19th century by the Reverend John Moore, who exposed the natural rock to great effect and planted many of the garden's majestic trees. His nephew, Hugh Armitage Moore, added a wide selection of botanical treasures, many introduced by Victorian plant hunters. Rowallane combines an array of garden forms: natural rock garden, formal walled garden, woodland dell, bog garden, semi-natural and natural landscapes. It has a unique collection of conifers and an outstanding range of acid-loving plants, particularly rhododendrons, hydrangeas and magnolias.

Saltram, Devon

A plantsperson's garden with a strong tradition of plant collecting. Sweeping lawns around the house give way to a network of paths that lead the visitor through the different areas of the garden. A formal lime avenue, about 80m long, is underplanted with narcissi. *Cyclamen hederifolium* carpet the ground in late summer. Rhododendrons, camellias and hydrangeas provide bold colour among the shrubberies, which shelter many interesting plants, including tender species from the southern hemisphere. The 18th-century orangery, Gothic castle and Fanny's Bower provide architectural and historical interest.

Scotney Castle, Kent

Scotney was laid out by Edward Hussey III from the late 1830s onwards. The landscape's design

Above · A view across the moat around Scotney Castle, Kent.

rejected the old-fashioned trends of formal and 'tidy' gardens, instead exemplifying the Picturesque style, set around the ruins of a 14th-century moated castle. Features include the Quarry Garden, which is home to ferns and heavily scented Ghent azaleas. The moat is fringed with yellow iris, rodgersia and kingcup. The parkland supports one of the UK's oldest hornbeam trees, which has been nominated for the Woodland Trust's Tree of the Year award.

Seaton Delaval Hall, Northumberland

Seaton Delaval was owned by the de la Val family from the early 12th century. The main gardens include a sunken rectangular garden laid out as a parterre by James Russell in 1950, enclosed by a ha-ha to the north-west and south-west. Gravel paths, a central fountain and box-edged parterres are flanked on either side by longer, narrower parterres. A parterre rose garden abuts the south-west wing of the hall, beside which is a semicircular lawn with a mature weeping ash in the centre. The design of the south-east garden has been reimagined to include elements of play, emulating the sense of fun of the 'gay Delavals', who were known for wild parties and practical jokes.

Sheffield Park and Garden, East Sussex

The first Lord Sheffield called in 'Capability' Brown to design this landscape and James Wyatt to design the Gothick house. The garden owes its beauty both to Brown's original design of 1775 and to the later efforts of A.G. Soames, who acquired the park in 1909 and spent 25 years adding many exotic trees and shrubs. The designed lakes, bridges and waterfalls recall the original vistas, enhanced by 20th-century additions, including conifer, birch, tulepo, mespilus and eucryphia.

Sheringham Park, Norfolk

Sheringham Hall is set within a landscape park designed by the notable landscape designer

Humphry Repton for the Upcher family. Work began on the park and house in 1813. Generations of the Upcher family used Repton's designs to continue shaping the garden and parklands, which are famous for their vast collection of rhododendrons and azaleas. The last owner, Tom Upcher, used to hold rhododendron champagne parties in the 1950s to show them off.

Shugborough Estate, Staffordshire

An innovative estate developed by brothers George and Thomas Anson with walled gardens, parkland walks and veteran trees, including a champion yew. The 18th-century park and garden landscape is studded with notable garden buildings and monuments, including one of the first Chinese garden houses in the UK. Opposite the hall on a man-made island is the Oak Arboretum. A passion of the former owner Lord Lichfield, the oak collection boasts many species planted by family members and visitors to the hall and includes an oak grown from an acorn taken from the White House lawn.

Sizergh, Cumbria

Sizergh Castle Garden is the focus of a nationally significant designed landscape, developed in phases by the Strickland family from the 13th to the 20th century. It contains a variety of features, garden styles and planting within a sequence of linked compartments from various periods that reached their ornamental zenith

Above · Woodland at Roundwood Quay and Fort at Trelissick, Cornwall.

in the early 1930s. The final and most comprehensive scheme, by Hayes of Ambleside and Keswick, introduced a much greater range of plants, focused on the outstanding limestone Rock Garden, home to stunning Japanese maples. Later additions include yew topiary and the Stumpery. The garden layout of the early 1930s survives largely intact.

Stourhead, Wiltshire

A Palladian house and world-famous landscape garden are set amid an extensive 2,650-acre parkland and estate. The designed landscape was created by Henry 'the Magnificent' Hoare, one of a small group of early 18th-century 'gentleman gardeners' who used their land to create a symbolic and personal circuit walk around a centrepiece lake. The original planting of the garden was undertaken by a team of 50 gardeners, who planted and tended beech, oak, sycamore, Spanish chestnut, ash and holm oak. When Stourhead first opened in the 1740s, it was described as 'a living work of art'.

Stowe, Buckinghamshire

Stowe is one of the largest gardens in the world, featuring over 40 temples and monuments, eight lakes and a garden of 250 acres set within a parkland estate of over 750 acres. It took over 300 years to create and is unique in having employed so many of the leading architects, landscape designers and sculptors of the age, working many years apart to create a single idealised landscape. Stowe is home to the Farey Oak, believed to be around 700 years old.

Tolpuddle, Dorset

Set beside the River Piddle, the village of Tolpuddle gained national attention in 1834 as the home of the Tolpuddle Martyrs, six farmworkers who defied the Unlawful Oaths Act to form a union and protest against their meagre wages. The workers were said to have met under a sycamore, a tree that still stands today and is now cared for by the National Trust.

Trelissick, Cornwall

Trelissick's intimate gardens are set away from the mansion and slope down to the River Fal. Shady walks and woodland are a setting for rare trees and shrubs, including extensive collections of rhododendrons and azaleas. The mild, moist climate is the perfect habitat for tree ferns. The Gilbert family undertook much of the planting throughout the 19th century, but the rare shrubs and plant collection were largely planted by Ida and Ronald Copeland after they bought the property in 1937.

Tyntesfield, North Somerset

Tyntesfield is a Grade I listed Victorian house in a Grade II* registered garden and extensive parkland. It was purchased in 1844 by William Gibbs, who commissioned the architect John Norton to remodel and expand the mansion. The formal garden and pleasure grounds extend to around 27 acres. The arboretum ('Paradise') displays cedars grown from seed collected in the Holy Land alongside a fine collection of other exotic trees. The gardens include further ornamental areas, such as the Rose Garden and aviary, as well as more functional elements, such as a croquet/tennis lawn and ha-ha. In the 1890s Antony Gibbs commissioned the Arts and Crafts architect Walter Cave to redesign the garden in the Renaissance style then fashionable. The gardens are infused with the Gibbs's religious faith but also reflect the importance of horticulture to a family that owed much of its success to fertiliser made from seabird guano.

The Vyne, Hampshire

The Vyne is surrounded by over 22 acres of formal and informal gardens and woodland walks that take in 400 years of history, from medieval fishponds to concrete military structures from the Second World War. The original gardens were designed around two cone-roofed summerhouses, thought to be the first garden buildings in Britain. One of the summerhouses survives, now set among gardens with later design elements that trace the site's history. The gardens boast a fine herbaceous border by horticulturist Graham Stuart Thomas, as well as the famous Hundred Guinea Oak.

Waddesdon Manor, Buckinghamshire

In 1874–89 Baron Ferdinand de Rothschild employed a French architect to build a French Renaissance-style manor house. The gardens were laid out by the landscape architect Elie Lainé. Trees with coloured leaves were favoured to provide highlights. The grand parterre features thousands of bedding plants, seasonal bulbs and tropical 'dot' plants. The Pulhamite artificial rockwork and the aviary are among the garden's splendid structures. Waddesdon's rich variety of trees includes giant sequoia, Chinese thuja and fan palm, as well as large groups of Austrian pine, planted to create natural windbreaks.

Wallington, Northumberland

Wallington covers over 300 acres in the heart of the Northumbrian countryside. Traces of the 18th-century design remain in the woodland walks and pools, overlaid by colourful Victorian additions. Unusually, the walled garden is half a mile from the house, reached by a walk through the 'wilderness'. A conservatory houses a wide range of tender and half-hardy plants. From the 1850s the Trevelyan family planted newly available exotic conifers, discovered in the New World. In 1891 Sir George Otto Trevelyan began a tradition of recording the planting date, girth, height and position of Wallington's trees.

Westbury Court Garden, Gloucestershire

Westbury Court is a walled Dutch-style water garden originally laid out by local gentleman Maynard Colchester and his nephew between 1696 and 1714. The garden was restored from dereliction by the National Trust from 1967, using detailed accounts and a contemporary bird's-eye view by Johannes Kipp. The holm oak at Westbury is 400 years old, one of many mature specimens that also include one of the tallest tulip trees in the UK. A formal parterre with topiary and historical planting gives good displays in summer.

Wimpole Estate, Cambridgeshire

The grounds of the estate were first enclosed in 1302 and they were laid out and later modified by a range of landscape designers, including

Above · An espaliered apple tree in flower in the walled garden at Wimpole, Cambridgeshire.

Charles Bridgeman, 'Capability' Brown and Humphry Repton. Bridgeman introduced a grand avenue, 2½ miles long, in the early 18th century, while the rest of the park is more Picturesque in style, with designed treescapes of clumps and individual specimens. The pleasure grounds contain an informal but international collection of ornamental trees and shrubs and a national collection of walnut trees. The restored walled garden includes glasshouses recreated from designs by Sir John Soane.

Winkworth Arboretum, Surrey

In 1938 amateur arborist Wilfred Fox cleared bracken and brambles to create an arboretum on a hillside in Surrey. Exotic trees have been planted among native trees to create a sense of wildness, echoing Chinese mountains and New England forests. An oak woodland and stream-fed lake at the base of the hill remain unchanged. The plantsmanship of Dr Fox shows in his addition of glades designed for winter interest and early spring colour, which he planted with both introductions and established species, such as rhododendrons, witch hazel, dogwood and magnolia specimens.

Woolsthorpe Manor, Lincolnshire

Woolsthorpe Manor was Isaac Newton's childhood home. Here he was inspired by nature and the Lincolnshire landscape, embarking on a lifetime of observation and inquiry. Newton returned to the manor from Cambridge University at the time of the Great Plague, and it was here that he began to develop his theories on gravity. The small garden includes an orchard of 'Flower of Kent' apple trees.

Compiled by National Trust garden teams and regional consultants

Overleaf · Trees were an essential element of Humphry Repton's landscape designs, including his scheme for Sheringham Park in Norfolk.

Index

Acknowledgements

The author is grateful to the countless members of National Trust staff who contributed to the production of this book. Sincere thanks to all the gardens advisers, gardeners and other property staff who suggested trees for inclusion. I'm sorry we couldn't include all the trees you nominated – it would have been an enormous tome if we had. Thank you for responding so quickly and enthusiastically to our many enquiries and requests for information, even when you were busy keeping our gardens looking fabulous. Special thanks to Tommy Teagle, Rosy Sutton, Heloise Brooke, Chris Skinner, Susan Rowley, Richard Marriott, Paul Walton and Charlotte Croft.

Thanks to Christopher Tinker, the National Trust's Publisher for Curatorial Content, for initiating the book, overseeing the editing, design and production, and for his constant attention to quality. I am also grateful to David Boulting, Editor in the Cultural Heritage Publishing team, for sourcing pictures, copy-editing the text and advising on content.

Pam Smith, Senior National Consultant for Gardens and Parklands, shared her enormous knowledge, compiled the gazetteer and helped greatly in liaising with staff in gardens and parks. Alison Crook, Plant Collections Curator, provided endless information on the whereabouts and details of trees; and Joanne Ryan shared her knowledge and pictures of the rhododendrons at Leith Hill.

Thanks to Megan Wheeler for valuable research and advice on the National Trust collections and links with trees and wood; Helen Antrobus and Elizabeth Green for reading and checking copy and making many useful suggestions; Andy Jasper, John Deakin and Tarnya Cooper for their wise thoughts on content and style; and Claire Masset for suggesting trees as a potential topic for this series.

I am also grateful to Tim Pye for researching illustrations of trees in our library collections; Matthew Hollow for his photography of botanical illustrations at Anglesey Abbey and James Baugh for assisting him; Matthew Young for his beautiful cover design; Patricia Burgess for proofreading the book so meticulously; Christopher Phipps for his index; and Richard Deal at Dexter Premedia for the origination.

The National Trust gratefully acknowledges a generous bequest from the late Mr and Mrs Kenneth Levy that has supported the cost of preparing this book through the Trust's Cultural Heritage Publishing programme.

Picture credits

Published in Great Britain by the National Trust, Heelis,
Kemble Drive, Swindon, Wiltshire SN2 2NA

National Trust Cultural Heritage Publishing

ISBN 978-0-70-780461-3

A CIP catalogue record for this book is available from the British Library.

10 9 8 7 6 5 4 3 2 1

Publisher: Christopher Tinker
Project editor: David Boulting · Proofreader: Patricia Burgess
Indexer: Christopher Phipps · Cover designer: Matthew Young
Page design concept: Peter Dawson, www.gradedesign.com
Colour origination by Dexter Premedia Ltd, London

MIX
Paper from
responsible sources
FSC
www.fsc.org   FSC® C114687

Printed in Wales by
Gomer Press Ltd on
FSC-certified paper

The cover images are based on illustrations from the following books held by
the Library at Anglesey Abbey, Cambridgeshire: *Dendrologia Britannica* (1825)
by P.W. Watson (NT 3124740); *Figures of the Most Beautiful, Useful, and Uncommon Plants* (1760) by Philip Miller (NT 3051104); *Histoire des Arbres Forestiers de l'Amérique Septentrionale*, vols. 1–3 (1810–13) by François André-Michaux
(NT 3101525); *The Spirit of the Woods* (1837) by Rebecca Hey (NT 3101594);
A Supplement to Medical Botany (1794) by William Woodville (NT 3124738)

Discover a wealth of great art, treasures and living collections
at National Trust places throughout England, Wales and
Northern Ireland. Visit the National Trust website:
www.nationaltrust.org.uk/art-and-collections
and the National Trust Collections website:
www.nationaltrustcollections.org.uk

Measurements are given in metric form except where
imperial units, such as miles and acres, will be more familiar
to UK readers (1 mile = 1.6 kilometres, 1 acre = 0.4 hectares)

THE AUTHOR

Simon Toomer is a forester, arboriculturist and botanist.
He is Curator of Living Collections at Kew Gardens and
was formerly Senior Consultant for Plant Conservation
with the National Trust and Director of Westonbirt, the
National Arboretum. He has written a number of books
and other publications and shares his knowledge of trees at
conferences and other public forums. He has travelled widely
in the pursuit of plants to study, photograph and collect.

ALSO AVAILABLE IN THIS SERIES

*125 Treasures from the
Collections of the National Trust*

ISBN 978-0-70-780453-8

*100 Paintings from the
Collections of the National Trust*

ISBN 978-0-70-780460-6